Professional Learning Communities
for Science Teaching

Lessons From Research and Practice

Professional Learning Communities *for* Science Teaching

Lessons From Research and Practice

Edited by Susan Mundry and Katherine E. Stiles
Foreword by Page Keeley

NSTA press
National Science Teachers Association
Arlington, Virginia

National Science Teachers Association

Claire Reinburg, Director
Jennifer Horak, Managing Editor
Judy Cusick, Senior Editor
Andrew Cocke, Associate Editor
Betty Smith, Associate Editor

ART AND DESIGN
Will Thomas, Jr., Director

PRINTING AND PRODUCTION
Catherine Lorrain, Director

NATIONAL SCIENCE TEACHERS ASSOCIATION
Francis Q. Eberle, Ph.D., Executive Director
David Beacom, Publisher

Library of Congress Cataloging-in-Publication Data
Professional learning communities for science teaching : lessons from research and practice / Susan Mundry and Katherine E. Stiles, editors ; foreword by Page Keeley.
    p. cm.
  Includes index.
  ISBN 978-1-935155-00-3
  1. Science--Study and teaching--United States. 2. Science teachers--In-service training--United States. 3. Professional learning communities--United States. I. Mundry, Susan. II. Stiles, Katherine E. III. National Science Teachers Association.
  Q183.3.A1P757 2009
  507.1--dc22
                        2009003259

NSTA is committed to publishing material that promotes the best in inquiry-based science education. However, conditions of actual use may vary, and the safety procedures and practices described in this book are intended to serve only as a guide. Additional precautionary measures may be required. NSTA and the authors do not warrant or represent that the procedures and practices in this book meet any safety code or standard of federal, state, or local regulations. NSTA and the authors disclaim any liability for personal injury or damage to property arising out of or relating to the use of this book, including any of the recommendations, instructions, or materials contained therein.

Table of Contents

Acknowledgments

We want to thank those who helped us build this collection of chapters that tell important "stories" in science education. Our focus on professional learning communities (PLCs) in science education brings together a diverse array of stories that have the potential to impact readers from diverse contexts and settings.

Page Keeley, 2008–2009 NSTA president, provided the leadership and vision for the theme of this book, and we gratefully acknowledge her contributions to the endeavor. Her foreword provides the overarching context that frames the authors' stories.

The authors of each chapter address the topic of PLCs from their own unique perspectives, and we gratefully acknowledge their contributions to the book as a whole. Each author graciously and thoughtfully responded to our suggestions for revisions, and we want to thank each of them. We also want to thank those staff in the authors' organizations who helped prepare their final manuscripts. We know that without our own administrative assistant, Deanna Maier, this book would not have come to fruition—thank you, again, Deanna.

NSTA staff, specifically Claire Reinburg and Jennifer Horak, deserve special recognition. Claire provided the opportunity for us to compile and edit this book, and Jennifer supported us throughout the editing and production process. We are also grateful to Will Thomas and Catherine Lorrain, for creating such an attractive book. Thanks to our copyeditor, Patricia Freedman, who did a tremendous job and attended to every detail needed to finalize the manuscript, as well as our proofreader, Andy Cocke.

And, finally, we want to thank our supportive families and our colleagues at WestEd, who continue to inspire us, support our contributions to education improvement, and enable us to do the work we love.

Susan Mundry and Katherine E. Stiles
Editors

Introduction

The "ideal" impact of this collection of stories would be for readers to develop a vision of PLCs in their own contexts and initiatives, glean the lessons learned from each story, and implement strategies that support teachers and schools to move toward becoming PLCs.

To support you, the reader, in this endeavor, we suggest the following reflection questions to help you engage with the "lessons learned" in Chapters 2–8:

- How is your context similar to and different from the one described in the chapter? How can you translate the contextual issues identified in the chapter into your own site? What structures exist within your context that both support and inhibit the implementation of PLCs?

- How would you describe your own culture (e.g., What are the norms for collaboration? How do people respond to change?)? What kind of culture existed in, or was developed, in the chapter? How close to, or far away from, that kind of culture is your organization? What would it take to move closer toward a culture that supports and sustains PLCs?

- Who is your audience (e.g., teachers, teacher leaders, administrators, higher education faculty, external consultants)? What can you learn from the chapter about how to involve and engage your audience in PLCs?

- What were the challenges faced by the chapter author(s)? How were the challenges overcome? What successes resulted? In what ways are the challenges similar to and different from those that you face? What can you learn from the solutions that were implemented?

- What are the big ideas or lessons learned from the chapter that can support you in your own efforts to implement PLCs? What can you take action on immediately? What do you need to do to enable you to institute other actions?

In addition to these reflection questions, Chapters 2–8 provide questions that expand on the themes identified here and help you reflect on your learning as it relates to the chapter's specific context and story about PLCs. To further enhance your own implementation of PLCs, the appendix provides information on resources available through the National Science Teachers Association and a description of a comprehensive website, All Things PLC, where you can find more information about developing PLCs.

Our goal in gathering this collection of chapters that tell the story of PLCs in a diversity of settings is to enhance readers' own efforts in building PLCs that strengthen science teaching and learning. We hope that through reading and reflecting on what you learned, we have achieved our goal.

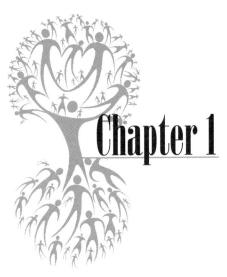

Chapter 1

The Promise of Professional Learning Communities

Susan Mundry and Katherine E. Stiles

"Community and leadership cannot occur if teachers remain isolated from each other. Departments and schools must institute policies and procedures that support teacher collaboration, risk taking, collegiality with other teachers as well as with experts outside of the school environment, and teachers taking on leadership roles within, and outside of, the school. Developing this community requires a recognition that professional learning is a lifelong process that is best nurtured within the norms and culture of the school."

—Susan Loucks-Horsley

Chapter 1

In this chapter we discuss the origin and the characteristics of professional learning communities (PLCs) and summarize the research findings on the impact and results achieved by schools that are organized as PLCs.

Rationale for PLCs

There is a growing recognition that teachers, like all professionals, need to continue to learn throughout their careers in order to stay current in their subject areas and teach an increasingly challenging curriculum to a diverse student body. To support teachers' engagement in lifelong learning, educational reform literature in the 1990s began calling for new organizational arrangements that support professionals to work in teams, use data and feedback on performance to make continuous improvements, and learn from practice (Astuto et al. 1993; Louis and Kruse 1995). Although many schools and districts began instituting changes that reflected the emergent emphasis on team approaches to teacher collaboration, the pressure to organize schools for maximum learning continues to increase. Educators are confronted with the questions "How do we respond when students do not learn?" and "What do we need to know and be able to do to reach all students?" and are attempting to implement a variety of strategies to put their response systems in place. One of the strategies schools and districts are using is to organize themselves into a *professional learning community*, a structure that supports teacher learning and continuous improvement that research literature suggests is a promising strategy for enhancing student outcomes (Lee, Smith, and Croninger 1995; Marks, Louis, and Printy 2000; Newmann and Wehlage 1995).

There are many arguments for building PLCs in schools: to increase coherence, to reduce isolation, to develop teacher knowledge, and to intervene early when students are in danger of failing. Education, like other organizations operating in the 21st century, must increasingly invest in and be able to rely upon its greatest asset—human capital—to achieve desired results. In the 19th and early 20th centuries, businesses invested in the "hard goods" of machinery and products; today's economies require greater investment in people—their knowledge, skills, and capacity. Human capital drives economic health by putting knowledge to work through the innovation, ingenuity, and ideas of people.

Schools are in a unique position with respect to building human capital. Business and industry rely on education to build what economists call the "general human capital" such as literacy and thinking skills, and schools are now being asked to support the development of skills that matter most for the 21st century—such as the ability to think creatively and to evaluate and analyze information. We believe it will be very hard to develop students with 21st-century skills unless the adults in schools (teachers and administrators) are given the opportunity to operate with a 21st-century perspective and have permanent structures for professional learning. PLCs show great promise for supporting schools to make the shifts in thinking and practice needed to succeed in the future.

As we have worked with science education leaders around the country we have seen, in place after place, that professional development has evolved from the "one-shot, learn something you can bring back to the classroom on Monday" mentality to one that appreciates and supports the dynamic nature and complexity of teaching and recognizes the challenges of developing all students to thrive in the 21st century. A quote often attributed to Charles Darwin comes to mind when we think about what is needed for the future: "It is not the strongest of the species that survives, nor the most intelligent that survives. It is the one that is the most adaptable to change." Although Darwin was talking about a very different kind of change, schools that are organizing as PLCs are becoming more adaptable to change because they are carefully examining results, assessing what is working, changing what is not, and providing the leadership to guide and support the new structures for learning.

The Origin of Learning Communities

In 1990, Peter Senge wrote a book called *The Fifth Discipline: The Art and Practice of the Learning Organization.* It was the first exposure many educators had to the idea that as the world shifted into the Knowledge Age, we would see fundamental changes in how workplaces were organized and how the people in them conducted their work. We must admit that while we applied Senge's work very early in schools involved in restructuring in the 1990s, it was difficult work and people struggled to implement these ideas because they required rethinking "sacred" beliefs about the school schedule, school leadership, and teacher autonomy. Yet many visionary educators persevered. They challenged the status quo and pushed for necessary change, and now they are successfully putting these ideas to use to fundamentally change "business as usual" in our nation's schools.

Senge predicted we would all work in organizations that promoted continuous learning. We would use data to see the big picture and monitor and adjust our actions to achieve greater results. We would examine our beliefs and assumptions and start to inquire into our practice with key questions like "Why are we doing this?" and "Why are we doing this, this way?" We would develop the disciplines needed to notice patterns of behavior in our organizations that were helping us, and also those that were defeating us. Each person would continuously develop "personal mastery" and generously share his or her knowledge with others. In learning organizations, people would become personally responsible and accountable and

commit to visions or clear purposes for the work. We would work in teams and value and celebrate the contributions of our teammates.

The PLCs or communities of practice of today have their roots in Senge's vision for learning organizations and have created the examples and existence proofs that make it possible to see how more schools can achieve the vision that Senge laid out almost two decades ago. The work of Etienne Wenger and colleagues (2002) has also influenced the form and function of PLCs. This work recognizes that in all types of knowledge work, such as work done in the education field, the people working in the field need to engage in social exchange, experimentation, and shared experiences to develop and share knowledge. In education, this would help us avoid islands of innovation, reduce waste of resources, and stop the constant reinventing of the wheel that we often see.

Wenger and colleagues identified the benefits of people working together in communities of practice, which would serve as systems for continuous learning. In communities of practice people are informally bound together by shared expertise and a common domain in which they have a great interest. The communities have three main characteristics: domain, community, and practice. Members engage in common work or discussion and help each other focus on the specific domain topic of their community. The members develop a shared practice with shared processes, knowledge, and resources. For example, among educators these shared practices might be particular approaches to examining student work or revising instructional materials, or ways they assess student learning. Being a part of the community of practice helps members build common language, methods, and models around specific topics. Major benefits of communities of practice are that they tend to reduce barriers and promote cross-fertilization and innovation and they can spread effective practices more rapidly (Wenger, McDermott, and Snyder 2002).

Communities of practice can exist on their own or be a part of larger PLCs where a subgroup of teachers may decide to focus in on a domain of interest to inform themselves and the wider community (e.g., a community of practice focused on teaching science inquiry or on using formative assessments). Increasingly, communication technologies and innovative cyber tools allow for people to collaborate in such communities of practice on products and ideas wherever they are located, and it is predicted that these online communities of practice will continue to grow in popularity and use.

What Are PLCs?

As we began to plan this book and invite authors to submit chapters based on their work, we asked ourselves what images of PLCs we wanted to portray. In canvassing colleagues and reviewing the literature, we realized that the purposes and characteristics of PLCs may look different from place to place but, like other professional development strategies, PLCs have necessary key components that define them. People working together on a task does not necessarily constitute a PLC. Hord and Sommers (2008) pointed out that PLCs are not just new ways of teachers working together on their tasks but rather are structures for continuous learning and use of knowledge in the course of conducting the work of teaching. The good examples we have seen in operation (such as the many described in this book) have this distinction: *teachers in every case are learning (e.g., new content, pedagogical content, models for infusing literacy into content, strategies for formative assessment, leadership skills) and working with their peers to situate their learning in real practice.*

We have been somewhat alarmed by teachers who tell us they have "mandatory PLC time" when they must come up with ways to drill students and make sure they pass the tests. In these situations, it seems the main purpose or idea for the PLC has been hijacked to perpetuate the same knee-jerk focus on short-term gains that have plagued schools these last few years. We ask, Who is learning in these situations? Instead of intellectual engagement, serious reflection on teaching and learning and teacher collaboration, these groups are grabbing at PLCs as the next silver bullet for meeting their quarterly or annual performance targets. From our work in professional development, we want to point out the danger of using PLCs this way.

PLCs are as much about a set of beliefs that take hold and a culture that develops as they are about the specific actions the PLC members take to improve student outcomes. PLCs at their core are results oriented (DuFour and Eaker 1998). They require a considerable amount of groundwork, including getting school principals engaged, building teacher leadership, creating the time and structure, and developing the interpersonal and analytical skills needed for them to be productive and successful.

As we noted earlier in this chapter, there are variations on what a PLC looks like from place to place but most have common characteristics. The term itself, *professional learning community,* helps to define what it is: a collective group of professionals learning together under certain specific conditions. However, the term can also lead to confusion; many people think any collaborative work becomes a PLC, and we have even heard a few people say they thought the learning had to be conducted out in the "community."

DuFour et al. (2006) defined six characteristics of PLCs:

1. *Focus on Learning.* The school is focused on and committed to promoting learning for students and teachers. The faculty develop and are guided by principles describing what they believe and what they hope to create. There is a commitment to and expectations that everyone will enact these principles every day to bring about desired student results. In the science classroom, for example, you might see how a school's principle of promot-

ing deeper learning and thinking for all students plays out when teachers immerse students in inquiry and spend significant time supporting students to develop explanations of science ideas and phenomena.

2. *Collaborative Culture Focused on Learning.* PLCs have collaborative teams that work interdependently to achieve shared goals. For example, teams of teachers and leaders work together to learn instructional strategies for increasing student learning. They work together to deepen their knowledge, apply their knowledge in the classroom, and come together to reflect on how their actions are improving lessons and learning; they then decide on the next steps for their learning.

3. *Collective Inquiry.* Staff engage in collective and public inquiry to ask, How are we doing? What do we need to learn next? How do we get better results? They demonstrate a commitment to continuous learning and continuous school improvement. For example, science faculty might review student results and discuss what they need to do about areas where student understanding is weak. They would refer to resources and research findings for ideas and suggestions to better address students' naive conceptions and promote learning. They would try out new strategies and continue to inquire into how new practices are working, making adjustments along the way as they learn more.

4. *Action Orientation and Experimentation.* PLCs are focused on learning and are organized so that teachers can take immediate action on their learning. A group of science teachers in a PLC may decide to get to know the *National Science Education Standards* (NRC 1996) better for the grades and topics they teach, but they don't stop there. They would immediately ask themselves, How does what we are learning influence our practice? and What are the applications to teaching and implications for action? This might lead them to fill in gaps in their instructional materials, institute the use of classroom assessments, increase the use of investigations, or infuse writing into the science classroom. They would take action quickly and then reflect again on results.

5. *Continuous Improvement.* In PLCs the status quo, even when results are "above the state average," is not good enough. Everyone commits to making continuous improvements and is expected to initiate and share improvements at every level. When asked, anyone in a school organized as a PLC can answer the questions "What have you improved lately?" and "Why did you improve it and what results have you seen?" They are also ready to share their interventions and findings with their colleagues so that others may quickly adopt changes that are working well.

6. *Results Orientation.* According to DuFour et al. (2006), the bottom line for PLCs is results. Teachers use multiple sources of data to assess how well

they are meeting goals for improved learning and measure their progress toward achieving specific goals. For instance, if the goal is to increase the number of students taking three or more years of science courses in high school, the school might monitor longer-term indicators such as changes in students' attitudes toward science in middle school and early high school, as well as outcomes such as enrollment data, to continually assess how the school is doing in its efforts toward meeting the goal and to take new actions as needed.

One characteristic implied but not explicitly stated in the discussion of these six characteristics defined by Dufour et al. is that schools organized and functioning as PLCs also make use of external resources. PLCs cannot exist in a vacuum; there must be knowledge-using and knowledge-producing avenues for the PLC members. *Knowledge using* means that the PLC members are consulting the latest research summaries, reading journals, and subscribing to online services that provide information on promising practices. *Knowledge producing* means that when they discover something that works, they document and share it within their own school and beyond.

Hiebert, Gallimore, and Stigler (2002) proposed that we need to develop a professional knowledge base for teaching that is similar to the knowledge bases in business, medicine, and law, which provide professionals in those fields with ready access to cases, research results, and legal decisions to inform decision making and practice. In education, members of PLCs would be primary consumers of such a knowledge base as well as potential contributors to it because schools organized as PLCs have structures for documenting and sharing their specialized knowledge. They often document via video and print what they are learning and how that influences student learning, with the intention of disseminating it to other teachers.

Many schools seeking to improve science education also use external resources such as scientists and higher education science faculty to bring content specialists and teachers together to focus specifically on improving science teaching. These external resources extend the boundaries of many PLCs to a whole community, region, and even a state.

In essence, PLCs are "communities of professionals caring for and working to improve student learning together by engaging in continuous collective learning of their own" (Hargreaves 2008, p. ix). The theme of "continuous, collective learning" must be a part of every PLC. In PLCs teachers and other staff have the structures to come together and engage in a continuous cycle of reflection and action, learning from their action and applying their learning and then reflecting again.

Hord and Sommers (2008, p. 9) examined extensive literature on PLCs and gleaned five attributes that define PLCs, some of which overlap with those identified by DuFour and colleagues (2006) as outlined earlier in this chapter:

1. *Shared Beliefs, Values, and Vision.* The staff share an "unrelenting attention to student learning success" (Hord and Sommers 2008, p. 10). They focus on *learning*—student learning as well as adult learning. As we like to ask teachers often, Who is doing the learning around here? In PLCs the answer is "everyone." The adults, as well as the students, are often asked, What did you learn today?

2. *Shared and Supportive Leadership.* The staff have shared power and authority for making decisions. Schools identify the responsibilities for decision making across the school and how decisions will be made.

3. *Collective Learning and Its Application.* In PLCs the staff continuously learn together and apply what they learn to their work (Hord and Sommers 2008, p. 12). They ask, What is working and how can we build on that? What isn't and how can we change that? They access outside resources, books, materials, and tools to propel themselves forward.

4. *Supportive Conditions.* PLCs need to provide for both *structural factors* to make sure teachers have the time, location, resources, leadership, and support to form a PLC and *relational factors* to support the members of the PLC to use the interpersonal skills needed to be open, honest, and caring contributors.

5. *Shared Personal Practice.* A hallmark of PLCs is that they bring educational practice into the public domain. Teachers observe and provide feedback to one another and examine student work to support improvement and growth. There is a collective understanding of the approaches, strategies, and tools that the school is using, and attention is paid to how well they are working and whether changes are needed.

Taken as whole, the early work of Senge and Wenger and colleagues and the more recent work of DuFour and colleagues and Hord and Sommers point toward a growing convergence of the kinds of structures and cultures in our schools that enhance learning for all and improvement in practice. These cultures are characterized by a focus on learning, collaboration among teachers, shared leadership, and a continuous emphasis on results and using reliable and research-based resources to guide improvement. Table 1.1 summarizes the differences in the structures and cultures between traditional schools and those that operate as professional learning communities.

Research on PLCs

There have been several comprehensive literature reviews that examined and summarized research on PLCs. Hord (1997) examined the research literature for evidence that the attributes of PLCs, including teacher collaboration, shared decision making among staff, and the practice of examining teaching and learning as a means to reform, showed positive outcomes. She reported on a study conducted

Table 1.1. Characteristics of Professional Learning Communities (PLCs)

Traditional School Structure	PLC
The culture is process oriented with a focus on teaching.	The culture is results oriented with a focus on learning.
Teachers work mostly in isolation, with some working together on tasks and ad hoc committees.	Teachers work together collaboratively and interdependently every day to learn, share practice, examine results, and enhance their work.
There are quarterly and end-of-year assessments to assign grades.	There is frequent assessment of results used to identify successes and needed improvements.
The vision comes from top leaders, or the vision/purpose is unclear.	The school's purpose and vision for learning are understood and shared by all.
There are a few central leaders.	The leadership is distributed among school staff.
Resources are mostly limited to instructional materials.	Resources include internal and external expertise, books, materials, and diverse tools and technology.
Teachers rarely have common planning time or other supports.	Teachers have time during the day to collaborate and access to professional development to enhance their interaction skills.
Islands of innovation exist in individual classrooms.	Innovative and effective practices are shared openly.

by the Center on Organization and Restructuring of Schools examining findings on 11,000 students enrolled in 820 secondary schools across the nation (Lee, Smith, and Croninger 1995). In the schools that were identified as having elements of PLCs,

> the staff had worked together and changed their classroom pedagogy. They engaged students in high intellectual learning tasks, and students achieved greater academic gains in math, science, history, and reading than students in traditionally organized schools…the achievement gaps between students from different backgrounds were smaller in these schools, students learned more, and, in the smaller high schools, learning was distributed more equitably…. Teachers and other staff members experienced more satisfaction and higher morale, that students dropped out less often and cut fewer classes and staff and students had lower rates of absenteeism. (Hord 1997, pp. 26–27)

Louis, Marks, and Kruse (1996) found two sets of conditions that contribute to a PLC: (1) structural conditions and (2) human and social resources. The structural conditions they identified include small school size, simple forms of school organization, formal time scheduled for teacher planning, and teachers having the power and discretion to make decisions about teaching and learning. The human

and social resources supporting PLCs they found to be most critical include an openness to innovation, supportive leadership, feedback on instructional performance, and opportunities for professional development.

In a recent comprehensive review of literature on PLCs, Feger and Arruda (2008) reported on a research review of 11 studies focused on PLCs conducted by Vescio, Ross, and Adams (2008), stating that "although… few studies move beyond self reports of positive impact" (p. 80), based on their analysis of the studies identified the researchers found evidence of change in teaching practice. Also noted was that this change included "some limited evidence that the impact is measurable beyond teacher perceptions" (p. 88). Researchers found that the teaching culture and collaboration improved and teachers became more focused on student learning than they were prior to implementation of PLCs. In addition, "the six [of the 11 studies reviewed] that included students' learning outcomes reported improved achievement scores over time, suggesting that PLCs can have system-wide change" (Feger and Arruda 2008, p. 12).

Hord (1997) also reported on research from the Center on Organization and Restructuring of Schools (Newmann and Wehlage 1995). This work comprises four complementary studies including multiyear longitudinal case studies, as well as survey methods and collection of student test data.

> The results showed that comprehensive redesign of schools, including decentralization, shared decision making, schools within schools, teacher teaming, and/or professional communities of staff, can improve student learning. Four interconnected factors leading to improved student outcomes were identified: student learning,…authentic pedagogy,…organizational capacity,…[and] external support. (Hord 1997, pp. 30–31)

As the use of PLCs as an organizing structure matures, there are many lessons to be learned and shared. The excellent website All Things PLC, described in the appendix to this book, provides information on results from schools using the PLC model. This data gathering and sharing should continue. In addition, further empirical research is needed to shed light on the specific impacts of PLCs and the conditions under which they are achieved. In fact, some of the chapter authors of this book are engaged in research on PLCs and are contributing to the growing knowledge base.

References

Astuto, T. A., D. L. Clark, A. M. Read, K. McGree, and L. deK. P. Fernandez. 1993. *Challenges to dominant assumptions controlling educational reform.* Andover, MA: Regional Laboratory for the Educational Improvement of the Northeast and Islands.

DuFour, R. and R. Eaker. 1998. *Professional learning communities at work: Best practices for enhancing student achievement.* Bloomington, IN: National Educational Service.

DuFour, R., R. DuFour, R. Eaker, and T. Many. 2006. *Learning by doing: A handbook for professional learning communities at work.* Bloomington, IN: Solution Tree.

Feger, S., and E. Arruda. 2008. *Professional learning communities: Key themes from the literature.* Providence, RI: Brown University. Available at *www.alliance.brown.edu/db/ea_catalog.php*

Hargreaves, A. 2008. Foreword. In *Leading professional learning communities: Voices from research and practice,* S. M. Hord and W. A. Sommers. Thousand Oaks, CA: Corwin Press.

Hiebert, J., R. Gallimore, and J. Stigler. 2002. A knowledge base for the teaching profession: What would it look like and how can we get one? *Educational Researcher* 31 (5): 3–15.

Hord, S. M., and W. A. Sommers. 2008. *Leading professional learning communities: Voices from research and practice.* Thousand Oaks, CA: Corwin Press.

Hord, S. M. 1997. *Professional learning communities: Communities of continuous inquiry and improvement.* Austin, TX: Southwest Educational Development Laboratory. Available at *www.sedl.org/pubs/catalog/items/cha34.html*

Lee, V. E., J. B. Smith, and R. G. Croninger. 1995. *Another look at high school restructuring: Issues in restructuring schools.* Madison, WI: Center on Organization and Restructuring of Schools, School of Education, University of Wisconsin—Madison.

Louis, K. S., and S. D. Kruse, eds. 1995. *Professionalism and community: Perspectives on reforming urban schools.* Thousand Oaks, CA: Corwin Press.

Louis, K. S., H. M. Marks, and S. Kruse. 1996. Teachers' professional community in restructuring schools. *American Educational Research Journal* 33 (4): 757–798.

Marks, H. M., K. S. Louis, and S. M. Printy. 2000. The capacity for organizational learning: Implications for pedagogical quality and student achievement. In *Understanding schools as intelligent systems,* ed. K. Leithwood, 239–265. Stamford, CT: Jai Press.

National Research Council (NRC). 1996. *National science education standards.* Washington, DC: National Academy Press.

Newmann, F. M., and G. G. Wehlage. 1995. *Successful school restructuring: A report to the public and educators.* Madison, WI: Center on Organization and Restructuring of Schools. (ERIC Document Reproduction no. 387925)

Senge, P. M. 1990. *The fifth discipline: The art and practice of the learning organization.* New York: Doubleday.

Vescio, V., D. Ross, and A. Adams. 2008. A review of research on the impact of professional learning communities on teaching practice and student learning. *Teaching and Teacher Education* 24: 80–91.

Wenger, E., R. McDermott, and W. Snyder. 2002. *Cultivating communities of practice: A guide to managing knowledge.* Boston: Harvard Business School Press.

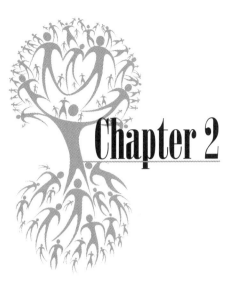

Chapter 2

"Late-Start Mondays":
The Catalyst for Change in an Urban High School
John W. Somers and Sandra Plyley

"The growth of any craft depends on shared practice and honest dialogue among the people who do it. We grow by private trial and error, to be sure—but our willingness to try, and fail, as individuals is severely limited when we are not supported by a community that encourages such risks."

—Parker Palmer, *The Courage to Teach* (1998, p. 144)

Chapter 2

Imagine this scene in a large urban high school: It is the first day of fall break and the school hallways are deafeningly silent. But, tucked away in an outer wing, building trades[1] and science teachers along with an instructional coach are collaborating to develop lesson plans and materials for a unit on mousetrap cars. The building trades teacher asks one of the science teachers to grab a hacksaw from the cabinet. After several minutes, the teacher sticks her head out and sheepishly asks, "What's a hacksaw?" The room erupts in respectful laughter. This collaboration between the Science Department and the Building Trades Program offers a glimpse into a thriving and unique professional learning community (PLC) at Ben Davis High School.

Background

Isolation, fragmentation, and privatization of teaching exist as the default culture in many urban high schools across the United States. Such a culture belies an organization whose primary purpose is learning. But the road map to creating a learning culture in schools is only now being drawn. The research and knowledge base has begun to yield a rich inside look at the characteristics and dynamics of schools that function as PLCs and the leadership necessary to establish and sustain them. At the high school level, the task of creating a whole-school community of practice is often monumental and requires tremendous energy to disrupt the status quo. The story that follows describes the process by which a large, urban high school formed a PLC focused on improving student results and promoting teacher learning and collaboration. Their guiding philosophy and approach was to create a *schoolwide* PLC rather than "islands of innovation" within different departments. For this reason, they identified student learning needs and teacher professional learning practices that spanned all grade levels and disciplines.

The PLC was constructed along three systems: assessment, data analysis, and student engagement. Teachers volunteered to serve as *strand leaders* to plan, model, and support professional development activities and to assist in the construction and analysis of common benchmark assessments. This chapter describes the innovative structure used for the PLC and discusses how the Science Department expanded its role by extending connections with middle school and elementary school teachers, engaging in cross-curricular work with building trades teachers, developing performance-based assessments, and showcasing lessons involving literacy strategies.

Origin and Evolution of the Ben Davis High School PLC

Ben Davis High School is located in the Metropolitan School District (MSD) of Wayne Township in Indianapolis, Indiana. The district has a total enrollment of

---

[1] The Building Trades program provides instruction in carpentry, electrical wiring, masonry, and related skills.

15,119 students (K–12); 52% of the student population are minorities and 64% qualify for free and/or reduced-price lunch. The high school has an enrollment of over 3,000 students in grades 10–12 and reflects the diversity of the district.

The springboard for the Ben Davis PLC is Late-Start Mondays. Each Monday morning, the faculty engages in 75 minutes of professional development focused on a number of issues related to teaching and learning and fostering student success. Strand leaders guide their colleagues through a host of focused conversations, which include infusing lesson plans with literacy strategies, creating common benchmark assessments, analyzing benchmark data, adjusting instructional practices, and studying an array of pedagogical approaches. The current principal of Ben Davis remarked that these 75 minutes have created space in which teachers can have deep and rich conversations about their teaching that has resulted in teachers "getting really good at understanding the craft of teaching and learning and taking ownership for student achievement." This outcome of practice-based learning has evolved over the last five years and has become a core value of the Ben Davis culture.

Establishing a schoolwide PLC in a large high school poses a unique set of challenges. Some of these challenges are associated with finding common time to meet and engage in sustained professional development given the sheer number of students and faculty; the coordination of classes, program choices, and teacher preparation periods; and the resulting compression of the instructional day. By contrast, elementary and middle schools are often able to exert greater control over their schedule and time because there is more homogenization of courses and program choices. The seemingly simple act of finding and scheduling a common period for the entire school to meet is frequently a structural challenge of starting any PLC (Hord and Sommers 2008). Despite this challenge, Ben Davis teachers and administrators envied the common planning time that the middle and elementary schools enjoyed and attempted to duplicate it at the high school level.

The most sensible place to start appeared to be by establishing small learning communities at a specific grade level in order to provide common planning time and to embark on creating a PLC. In the late 1990s, Ben Davis established five small learning communities at the 10th-grade level in which teams of teachers were responsible for specific groups of students; these teachers had an extra preparation period to share and develop common learning goals, assessments, and lesson plans and to address individual student issues and difficulties. Although this arrangement conferred benefits, the administrative leadership team wanted to expand the concept to the entire school. As a former principal of Ben Davis remarked, "We knew where we wanted to go, but we didn't know how. And we wanted to know what was different about how adults function in a schoolwide learning community— how do we get to the place where teachers can have powerful conversations about the art and science of teaching and learning?" Although common time was found

for teachers to meet when the five small learning communities were established at Ben Davis, this structure only addressed grade-level issues and did not promote whole-school collaboration. Teaming can give rise to "pockets of excellence" but can have a negative effect on promoting schoolwide culture.

By the late 1990s, education leaders began suggesting that a community of practice (Wenger n.d.) or a PLC (DuFour 2004) was a viable strategy for school-wide and organizational improvement. This idea was appealing to school reform-ers because both of these strategies provide a process through which individuals come together to form an intentional community in order to engage in collective learning with a focus on enhancing performance. At Ben Davis, that performance or outcome was both teacher and student learning. However, putting a PLC into practice in a high school presents a formidable challenge because the default culture in education is one of isolation (Wagner and Kegan 2006).

As a first step, a Ben Davis leadership team composed of teachers and the principal visited Adlai E. Stevenson High School in Lincolnshire, Illinois, and con-sulted with Richard DuFour, who, as the principal of Stevenson, had established a successful PLC. The goal for the leadership team's visit to Stevenson High School was to witness the interactions of teachers during their content team meetings. They looked at how the agenda was developed, the leadership of the meetings, and, most importantly, the interaction between teachers. They saw how teachers discussed, collaboratively, the results of common assessments. The Ben Davis lead-ership team was also very interested in Stevenson's program of student interven-tions. Their "pyramid" model scaffolded the types of educational supports students received based on escalating needs. Overall, the team was able to see how Steven-son High School functioned under their version of a PLC, and it sparked excellent discussion among the Ben Davis teachers as the team designed its PLC. From these observations and continuing conversations, book studies, and midnight musings, the principal proposed a "radical idea"—Late-Start Mondays—to the superinten-dent in 2003.

The idea of Late-Start Mondays was to delay the start of school each Monday for 75 minutes to provide time for the teachers to engage in professional develop-ment. As could be expected, transportation was one of the biggest hurdles to con-front, but after negotiation with the central office, the idea received a "go." Students would begin school at 8:45 a.m. rather than 7:30 a.m., and bus schedules would be adjusted to reflect this change. Instructional time was not affected because Ben Davis was already operating on an extended-day schedule. The only caveats from the superintendent were to ensure that the initiative was well organized and that it resulted in raising student achievement.

In fall 2004, an action committee was formed to study the formation and implementation of Late-Start Mondays. The committee comprised a cross section of high school personnel and community members. Creating Late-Start

Mondays was risky because it had far-reaching ramifications for internal and external audiences. For the internal audience of teachers, it meant a change in "how we do business around here"—how work would be organized, how learning would occur, what would be learned, how one's knowledge base and belief system might be challenged by others, and how some teachers would be thrust into new and perhaps uncharted leadership roles. For the principal, it meant sharing power, defining new boundaries and cultural expectations, forging and sustaining a focus on student learning and problems of practice, championing the cause, and negotiating and confronting opposition (Hord and Sommers 2008; Wagner and Kegan 2006). For the central office, it required locating new resources, removing barriers to implementation, supplying teachers with timely student learning data, and possibly reassigning personnel and/or hiring consultants to support professional development. For external audiences, primarily parents, it meant a change in schedule with possible transportation and work implications and evaluating the educational merit of this change. For the action committee, it required mustering the political will and skill to sell the idea to teachers and community members, the foresight to make smart moves, and the logic to organize the initiative in an efficacious manner. Most, if not all, of these issues confront any systemic change and restructuring initiative. The committee guided their initial actions with the following questions:

- What would late-start look like?
- How does it fit into the daily and weekly schedule?
- What would teachers accomplish?
- How do we provide accountability?
- What arrangements would be needed for bus schedules?

The school already had a strong spirit of cooperation with the central office, but the leadership team knew they needed to develop buy-in with other stakeholders, especially parents and teachers, and thus they held two community forums in spring 2005. At the forums they presented the rationale for late-start and the potential benefit to students, and they addressed questions carefully. The stakeholders unanimously endorsed the idea, and the initiative was to be launched in the fall. The administrators and instructional coach were not totally surprised at the ease of this acceptance, because both Ben Davis and the MSD of Wayne Township have a strong track record of reaching out and partnering with their community and stakeholders.

Given the green light, the high school leadership team worked through the summer to plan how they would use the shared learning time. They determined that the 75 minutes each Monday morning would be committed to creating opportunities for teachers to meet and collaborate and to engage in meaningful

Chapter 2

conversations. In general, the shared time would be devoted to department and team meetings, professional development, course meetings, common assessment development and analysis, and occasional staff meetings. They knew that professional development would drive change and that these sessions needed to be the focal point. They decided that professional development sessions would occur once per month and involve the entire faculty. To consolidate and manage planning, an instructional coach and assistant principal took charge of the Late-Start Mondays initiative. Table 2.1 provides a Late-Start Mondays schedule showing the various kinds of meetings.

The leadership team saw the role of formal professional development as the linchpin of success for Late-Start Mondays. Their foresight now comports with current literature in that one of the lessons learned in whole-school change is the need for school leaders to determine and guide the professional development in order for it to be anchored in raising student achievement and changing teacher practice (National Association of Secondary School Principals 2004). Therefore, the selection of topics must be intentional and mindful of the ultimate outcome—increasing student learning through effective instruction. Moreover, in order to disrupt the status quo, professional development must be simultaneously functional and transformational—that is, it must connect with classroom practice, provoke reflection on beliefs about learning and practice, embody the principles of change theory, and be in force over time.

The literature indicates that "deep change occurs only when beliefs are restructured through new understandings and experimentation with new behaviors" (Loucks-Horsley et al. 2003, p. 49). This quote points out the critical need for teachers to be able to take what they have learned from professional development and employ it in a psychologically safe environment where progress is measured incrementally and social support is provided for the construction of new meaning. On his website, Wenger speaks to this need for deep change when he states that "in the education sector, learning is not only a means to an end: it [is] the end product. The perspective of communities of practice is therefore also relevant at this level. In business, focusing on communities of practice adds a layer of complexity to the organization, but it does not fundamentally change what the business is about. In schools, changing the learning theory is a much deeper transformation." A PLC needs time to transform thinking and actions.

The Late-Start Mondays team decided early on that teachers would lead and facilitate the professional development. The instructional coach remarked that "teachers want to be taught by other teachers." The planning team made that principle a reality and took the initiative to recruit and "grow" teacher leaders in the building. These teachers represented the various content areas and received no other compensation than the opportunity to work with their colleagues. The decision to endorse teachers first and foremost as strand leaders comports with Wenger's ideal

Table 2.1. Late-Start Mondays Schedule of Meetings

August 20	Faculty meeting	January 7	Faculty meeting
August 27	Department meetings	January 14	Department meetings
		January 28	Course meetings
September 10	Course meetings		
September 17	Graduation exam meeting (GQE)	February 4	Shared learning
September 24	Shared learning	February 11	Department meetings
		February 25	Course meetings
October 1	Department meetings		
October 8	Course meetings	March 3	Department meetings, GQE
October 15	Shared learning	March 10	Course meetings
October 22	Department meetings	March 17	Shared learning
October 29	Course meetings	March 24	Department meetings
November 5	Shared learning	April 7	Course meetings
November 12	Department meetings	April 14	Shared learning
November 19	Course meetings	April 21	Department meetings
November 26	Shared learning	April 28	Course meetings
December 3	Department meetings	May 5	Shared learning
December 10	Course meetings	May 12	Share Fair—celebration
December 17	Faculty meeting	May 19	Faculty meeting

Department meetings are designed for entire departments to collaborate and share on the following topics: common assessments and collection of data, failure rates and interventions, use of reading strategies, curriculum mapping, engagement strategies, etc. *Course meetings* are designed for teachers of common courses to collaborate on the following topics: common assessments and inferences from data, intervention strategies, implementation of reading strategies, creation of core academic vocabulary activities and games, unwrapping the standards, etc. *Shared learning* meetings are designed for teachers to learn, practice, and share the successes and struggles of the current professional development.

of how a community of practice should function. On his website, Wenger states that "members of a community of practice are practitioners. They develop a shared repertoire of resources: experiences, stories, tools, ways of addressing recurring problems—in short a shared practice. This takes time and sustained interaction." A teacher can naturally address this peer-to-peer professional development process and translate the professional development content into applied practice.

Teacher leaders were supported in their new role by attending professional development institutes on effective instructional frameworks and strategies for improving student learning and then engaging other teachers in learning about them through the Monday-morning sessions. The teacher leaders were also supported with help from a consultant from a local university and district instructional coaches. To date, teacher leaders or strand leaders who are responsible for leading sessions during the shared learning time commit to being absent from their classrooms one day per month: a half-day to meet with the consultant and another half-day to meet with the instructional coach in order to prepare for the Monday-morning professional development sessions. The administration covers the classes with substitutes but staggers the periods so that the teachers do not repeatedly miss the same class. To bring other teachers into the fold, teacher leaders rotate on a periodic basis. This strategy works as a mechanism to build capacity throughout the school by including teachers in different content areas and departments.

Teachers choose areas of focus for their professional learning and attend multiple sessions on the same topic each semester in order to develop deep understanding. Each session progressively deepens the teacher's knowledge base and level of application. Such sophistication is necessary because the teachers are committed to exploring the various strategies learned through the professional development and expected to collaborate with other teachers, develop and implement lessons, and meet with department colleagues to share lessons and products. Some of the session topics for the last four years are listed in Table 2.2.

This first year of the schoolwide Late-Start Mondays needed to see a bright light of success and excite teachers about learning and trying new ideas in their classrooms. The effort also needed to promote the benefit of collaboration and having sustained conversations about teaching and learning, which could translate into student achievement. To manage the cultural impact, Late-Start Mondays for the first two years were mandatory—teachers had to sign attendance rosters and provide written feedback. An administrator was assigned to each session to ensure appropriate oversight and to be a part of the process. This strategy may appear heavy-handed, but it was a signal to the existing culture that "the way we do business around here" was changing. According to Schein (2008), establishing a learning culture requires intentional acts of leadership. He stated that "it can be argued that the only thing of real importance that leaders do is create and manage culture" (p. 362). At this early stage of implementation, school leaders needed to

Table 2.2. Shared Learning Topics for Late-Start Mondays

Academic Year	Shared Learning Topics (teachers select one)
2005–2006	Building a Positive Learning Environment Graphing Calculators 6+1 Writing Traits Reading for the Struggling Learner Strategies for Struggling Learners Beyond Reading Writing is a Process Cultural Competency 7 Keys to Reading Comprehension
2006–2007	Visualization Making Connections Determining Most Important Information Summarize and Synthesize Asking Questions Making Inferences Setting a Purpose Monitor and Clarify
2007–2008	Implementation of Reading Comprehension Strategies From 2006–2007
2008–2009	Literacy for New Teachers Beginning With the End in Mind (unit plans) Project-Based Learning

demonstrate that they were making a serious investment in establishing a learning organization with accountability and were willing to assume the responsibility for managing it to fruition.

In addition to professional development sessions, the 75 minutes on Monday were also used to provide time for departments to develop and refine common assessments, to analyze student learning based on these assessments, and to determine interventions for students who were receiving a failing grade. Ben Davis had been tracking the failure rate of students for over a year and intervening with a number of effective strategies (Reeves 2006). In 2007, the principal challenged the departments to take a closer look at the failure rate, discuss current interventions, and develop some new ideas. The results were quite impressive. The schoolwide failure rate decreased from 16% in spring 2006 to 6.5% in 2007–2008. According to teachers and administrators, some of this reduction can be traced back to focused conversations regarding individual students during the shared learning time and the prevalent use of literacy strategies. The Science Department in particular realized a decrease in the failure rate from 9.7% in 2006–2007 to 7% in 2007–2008. That decrease affected about 170 students, which means that these students turned failure into success.

Wagner and Kegan (2006) identified the seven disciplines for strengthening instruction—the first one is "urgency for instructional improvement using real data"

(p. 27). They noted schools that often generate too much data, which can overwhelm teachers; it might be better to use a single point of data such as the failure rate to send a powerful message. In the case of Ben Davis, their focus on one set of data as an indicator of success certainly proved to be a powerful message. Teacher discussions on Monday mornings were instrumental in keeping the focus on student learning and challenging teachers to turn student failure into student success.

A challenge to any PLC is the acculturation of new teachers in its attendant goals, beliefs, and practices. The current principal of Ben Davis remarked that they try hard to retain teachers so that they do not lose momentum, but a mechanism must exist to induct new teachers into the learning culture. Ben Davis had 32 new teachers at the start of the 2008–2009 school year, which illustrates this challenge. The principal added that they must differentiate their support for new teachers to help them become a part of the culture. Two teachers from chemistry and life science who have served as strand leaders for three years echoed the principal's point. They noted that they must work very diligently and deliberately with first-year and new teachers to challenge them to think about how to work with each other. The teachers stated that collaboration does not come naturally and the expectation to engage in dynamic conversations about teaching and learning requires risk taking, trust, and knowledge of the culture. Therefore, first-year and new teachers face a steep "change curve." In addition, the strand leaders pointed out that first-year teachers in particular have difficulty determining what information is most important to use in lesson planning, let alone deciding how to use the strategies to motivate students and optimize their learning.

Given the issues of acculturation and differentiating support, the Monday-morning collaboration time now consists of three levels. Level 1 is for first- and second-year teachers, who receive professional development in the basic literacy framework and strategies. Such strategies include how to increase reading comprehension, build and strengthen core academic vocabulary, and enhance writing fluency and thinking skills. Level 2 is for teachers who choose to revisit or explore further unit and lesson design. These teachers may decide to refine and practice the use of specific instructional strategies such as how to better activate and build background student knowledge. Level 3 is for experienced teachers who have been immersed in the PLC and want to move into new areas. The principal referred to this last phase as deep implementation—that is, teachers taking ownership of their own learning. For 2008–2009, the new area is project-based learning (PBL).

The Buck Institute for Education (2003) defines PBL as "a systematic teaching method that engages students in learning knowledge and skills through an extended inquiry process structured around complex, authentic questions and carefully designed products and tasks" (p. 4). The push for PBL grew from some of the nascent cross-curricular projects that involved several science teachers and other content areas such as English and building trades. About 90 teachers are currently involved in PBL activities. The teachers are free to choose partners, but they must declare the topic of their PBL and commit to creating a unit. Some of the projects that involve science teachers include "Alternative Fuels," in which students will create a bio-diesel engine; "Energy Transfer of the Human Body"; "How Can Understanding Chemistry Help You Improve the Water That You Use?"; and "Concrete and Chemistry."

Hord and Sommers (2008) addressed the need for teachers to share personal practice through classroom visits, observations, providing feedback, and interacting with each other around a common instructional practice. Such personal involvement builds positive relationships, which engender trust, collegiality, and sharing. Although the PLC at Ben Davis has not yet taken this personal path, they did create a whole-school experience in which teachers showcased their accomplishments. In spring 2008, the departments celebrated the professional development initiatives that they had been working on over the year by putting on a Share Fair. Each department made tri-fold boards and presented examples from their work. The boards included lesson plans, student work, pictures, and student data. Boards were exhibited in the school gymnasium, and faculty were given time to visit each other's displays. The leadership team felt that the Share Fair was a way to honor and celebrate the hard work that teachers had been doing. One of the life science teachers pointed out that "so many teachers around here are doing so many wonderful things and they have a lot to share."

Science Initiatives

The Science Department has a strong departmental PLC, but it has become more robust as a result of the conversations and shared learning time in Late-Start Mondays. A chemistry teacher remarked that "Monday mornings have influenced how we interact and how we purposively integrate literacy into our lessons." Within the last year, the Science Department has spearheaded several new collaborations and projects. The first one extended the PLC concept vertically by making connections with the elementary and middle school teachers.

The connection with elementary schools occurred as a result of district data indicating that students were not adequately prepared for the advanced curriculum of high school science. According to the district coordinator for math and science, students in grades 3–8 needed additional assistance in meeting the standards that address inquiry as well as science concepts and processes. She saw an opportunity to build on previous connections that the high school Science Department had made with the elementary schools. As a result, the district coordinator sent a survey to all elementary and middle school teachers to identify which state science standards they would like to learn more about. The elementary teachers responded very

positively to the survey and indicated a desire to deepen their content knowledge around a number of the state standards. They also wanted ideas about how best to teach these specific standards to students through an inquiry-based approach. This information was shared with the high school teachers, and they each selected a topic of focus for their work. They reviewed the district science curriculum guide and put together several inquiry-based lessons using hands-on activities that could be implemented in the elementary classroom.

In order to share these lessons and activities and additional topics relevant to the science curriculum, the high school science teachers organized a Teacher-to-Teacher Conference in March 2008 for K–8 teachers. The workshop topics included "Genetics Made Easy and DNA Extraction," "Magnetism and Electromagnetism," and "Vibrations, Waves, and Sound.'" The high school teachers expressed their excitement and desire to promote science instruction at the elementary level. Building on this momentum, the high school science teachers held an additional Share Fair for fourth-grade students from a local elementary school by having Advanced Placement students present for 10 minutes on a host of subjects (e.g., sharks, chemical reactions, elements and compounds, polymers, and phases of the moon). This fair served as another avenue to interest elementary students in science and to promote more vertical connections. The high school science teachers and the elementary teachers enjoyed partnering with each other to strengthen their students' science content knowledge.

For 2008–2009, the district has formalized four after-school sessions for high school science teachers and fifth- and sixth-grade teachers to engage in workshops, and one additional session to continue discussion about curriculum articulation. The central office administrator for math and science commented that the elementary teachers really enjoyed coming over to the high school to engage with the high school teachers. Obviously, the notion of an open community of learning permeates the district, and the willingness of the high school teachers to share their expertise makes this interaction a win-win situation, especially for students.

Another very interesting and innovative project took place in spring 2008. The genesis of this project grew out of the Monday-morning conversations and sessions. One morning the Integrated Chemistry/Physics (ICP) teachers were talking about how to help their students make connections and engage with the content. A building trades teacher overheard the conversation and interjected that perhaps some real-world connections might help. This conversation led the ICP and building trades teachers to sit down, compare each subject's state curriculum and standards, and look for overlaps. They wanted to see how they could create interdisciplinary lessons, bring more relevance to ICP students, and explore the possibility of awarding science credits through the building trades classes since the departments share some of the same students. Because of the need to ensure that state science standards would be met through the building trades curriculum, the last idea is still percolating. However, these conversations paid big dividends and led to the development of a PBL unit on electricity in the ICP classes entitled "The Household Wiring Unit." The building trades teacher worked with the ICP teachers on the practical aspects of household wiring and built stud walls in the ICP lab. The ICP teachers visited the house under construction by the building trades students to better understand the electrical and wiring process. Additionally, the ICP teachers spoke with the local power company to understand the process by which electricity is generated so they could convey this information to students. Students were challenged to take what they had learned about electricity in the ICP class and apply it by wiring a stud wall with a functional switch and socket. Specifically, the students had to develop a circuit, identify electrical devices, use materials and tools, and explain the flow of current in the circuit. The video of the unit showed a high degree of student engagement, learning, and enthusiasm. One of the ICP teachers remarked that the students certainly showed more effort and were quite willing to accept the challenge. She also commented that "returning to traditional instruction seemed so odd given the success of the applied unit." The building trades teacher exclaimed that the dual lesson was a "big win" and added that he only affects about 80 students a year in the Career Center, but now he had affected 800 students in ICP.

Another collaboration between the building trades and ICP teachers centered on the construction of mousetrap cars. Constructing mousetrap cars is a common activity in middle and high school classes to address national and state science standards associated with Newton's law, energy, acceleration, friction, and force (see Indiana's Academic Standards for Principles of Integrated Chemistry-Physics C.P.1.20-1.23 at *www. indianastandards.org/standard.asp?Subject=sci&Grade=CP&Standard=1*). The scenario at the beginning of the chapter occurred when the teachers were deciding how to approach this unit and build interdisciplinary content. The ICP teachers remarked that they could buy mousetrap car kits but did not want to do that. Instead, they teamed up with building trades teachers. An interesting development in this shared unit was how the teachers integrated writing. They decided that the students would supply some of the materials for the cars, such as axles. To obtain the necessary materials, the ICP students were required to submit a written requisition form. This form would contain all of the data needed to fulfill the order, such as the length of the axles. If the form was not legible or understandable, the form would be returned to the sender for clarification. This requirement illustrates the infusion of literacy into shared projects and how Ben Davis teachers strive to enact the professional development initiative.

The diffusion effect of Late-Start Mondays is emerging in the linkages between the Science Department and other content areas. Currently, English and science teachers have teamed up on a project-based unit, with more cross-curricular projects in the works. The exciting part of the Ben Davis story is not only what it has accomplished in a brief period of time, but also what the future holds for continued collaboration and creativity.

Lessons Learned

Reflecting on the process by which Ben Davis High School implemented its PLC yields some important insights. Foremost, change was driven through a top-down, bottom-up leadership process. School administration set the structure and institutionalized time in the school schedule for teacher learning. They outlined the expectations, but teachers led the professional development. This joint action by teachers and administrators not only was an effective strategy to achieve buy-in and accountability but also sent a powerful message of unity and commitment. Securing the support of external and internal constituents increased the supportive conditions necessary to launch the change effort. Such support reduces potential conflict and keeps the energy level high as the team builds the organizational infrastructure. Ben Davis also decided to take the PLC schoolwide, instead of by grade level or department, thus creating a culture of practice that cut across all content areas. This strategy provided opportunities for cross-curricular collaboration and assisted in reducing isolation. The Late-Start Mondays team employed a professional development theme of literacy strategies, which could be universally applied across content areas and result in increased student engagement, learning, and thinking. It also served as the catalyst for cross-departmental collaboration among teachers, further contributing to the schoolwide changes in culture. The school also found a way to celebrate their achievements by implementing low-cost Share Fairs, which gave all teachers an opportunity to showcase their hard work and results.

In most change efforts there are varying degrees of resistance and reasons for such opposition. In the case of Ben Davis, there was noted reluctance to engage in implementing professional development initiatives in the elective classes such as family and consumer sciences, physical education, music, and technology education. Most of these classes are performance-based classes, and these teachers did not understand how to apply the instructional strategies to their classrooms. All of the examples given in the professional development sessions were academic examples, and, until teacher leaders and administrators realized that they needed to sit down and talk with some of these elective teachers to help them with the connections, the teachers struggled. After the teacher leaders and administrators recognized this issue and provided feedback and the freedom to be creative with the strategies, in addition to more time to figure out how to fit the strategies into their curricula, these teachers became less resistant.

Another issue that sheds light on how PLCs evolve is the range of implementation of practice among the faculty. During the first year of the PLC at Ben Davis, the range of implementation was quite uneven, but subsequently more teachers in more content areas have come on board and endorsed the intent of the community to collaborate, de-privatize their teaching, and infuse their practice with a host of student-centered strategies. In addition, many teachers at Ben Davis have started to find others who share passions and ambitions in certain areas of the professional development (for example, PBL) and have forged ahead with their own additional learning. The PLC needs to provide flexibility for teachers at all levels of experience to identify their needs and personalize their learning.

A final lesson learned is the ongoing challenge to find ways to document continuous improvement and the success of the PLC toward its ultimate outcome—student learning. To be frank, Ben Davis continues to struggle with how to collect data to look at the success of its Late-Start Mondays. They continue to conduct staff and student surveys, experiment with walk-through data collection protocols, and use Literacy Audits to document strategy implementation data. True success will be seen in student achievement indices such as graduation rates, standardized test scores, student attendance records, and failure rates.

Based on the experiences at Ben Davis, if you are starting the PLC journey in your own context, here are some recommendations to keep in mind and some potential pitfalls to consider:

- Create a small leadership team with the authority to plan and coordinate the PLC goals, structure, calendar, and professional development. Include the person in charge of the master schedule on this team to plan and negotiate calendar challenges.
- Spend the time and money to develop teacher leaders and do so a year in advance of starting to implement changes in the school. Use your academic coaches to assist in this process.
- Build in time for continued professional development and learning throughout the school year. Make a commitment to establish protected time each week for teacher and team collaboration.
- Establish a system of accountability, and make expectations realistic and explicit. Monitoring attendance at PLC meetings sends a powerful message to the culture.
- Create time and structures that enable teachers to see each other in action in their classrooms. Provide teachers with opportunities to learn the skills and strategies for interactive dialogue and self-reflection.
- Plan well! Plan the first year in detail, with an outline of the next two to three years so that teachers and leaders know where they are headed.
- Start small and take baby steps toward achieving your vision.
- Build in time to celebrate success.
- Be sure to have flexibility in place, and be sure your plan has room for growth. From year to year, teachers will learn at different rates, and some teachers may need longer to implement strategies whereas others may

Chapter 2

master them quickly and need additional learning. In addition, make sure to plan for teachers who are new to the school. Ben Davis has hired more than 30 teachers over the last two years, and each needed his or her own opportunities to learn from the beginning.

- It is easy to share the successes, but don't be afraid to talk about the frustrations and struggles that are experienced. Sometimes the best way to move forward is to allow time to share frustrations and to find collaborative solutions.

Intended and Unintended Consequences

As Margaret Wheatley (2002) reminded us, conversation is powerful. As the authors were interviewing teachers and administrators, the word *conversation* kept coming up. Monday mornings were repeatedly referred to as the "time when we have conversations about teaching and learning." The teachers and administrators have capitalized on the power and courage of conversation to build a learning culture in their building. Sawyer (2007) contended that the genius of collaboration resides within the group and creativity is unleashed through the act of improvisation. He observed that "in both an improv group and a successful work team, the members play off one another, each person's contributions providing the spark for the next. Together, the improvisational team creates a novel, emergent product" (p. 14). The teachers, strand leaders, and administrators at Ben Davis showed the interplay of working as an improv team where ideas bounce off one another, creating breakthrough thinking, new designs, and interdisciplinary projects. That feeling was present during the interviews, watching the videos of PBL teams, and listening to the ICP and building trades teachers discuss the unit on mousetrap cars. If improvisation is the mark of a high-performing PLC, Ben Davis High School certainly embodies that distinction.

Reflection Questions

- What is your rationale for considering a PLC? What are the costs and benefits to teachers, students, and stakeholders?
- What variables in your context must be considered in order to plan and initiate a schoolwide PLC?
- How can leadership build on existing organizational strengths to effect change and build a community of practice?
- What internal and external resources are available to assist in planning and supporting schoolwide changes and initiatives?
- What district and school structures will support or hamper effective implementation of a PLC?
- What is the role of the central office in planning and supporting a PLC?

- How can resources be aligned across the school and district to support a PLC?
- Who are the potential teacher leaders and what is their level of expertise to initiate and sustain a PLC?
- What are your critical indicators of progress and success?

References

Buck Institute For Education. 2003. *Project based learning handbook: A guide to standards-focused project based learning for middle and high school teachers.* 2nd ed. Hong Kong: Quinn Essentials Books and Printing.

DuFour, R. 2004. What is a "professional learning community"? *Educational Leadership* 61 (8): 6–11.

Hord, S. M., and W. A. Sommers. 2008. *Leading professional learning communities: Voices from research and practice.* Thousand Oaks, CA: Corwin Press.

Indiana Department of Education. Indiana academic standards and resources. *www.indianastandards.org*

Loucks-Horsley, S., N. Love, K. E. Stiles, S. Mundry, and P. Hewson. 2003. *Designing professional development for teachers of science and mathematics.* 2nd ed. Thousand Oaks, CA: Corwin Press.

National Association of Secondary School Principals. 2004. *Breaking ranks II: Strategies for leading high school reform.* Reston, VA: National Association of Secondary School Principals.

Palmer, P. 1998. *The courage to teach.* San Francisco: Jossey-Bass.

Reeves, D. 2006. Leading to change: Preventing 1,000 failures. *Educational Leadership* 64 (3): 88–89.

Sawyer, K. 2007. *Group genius: The creative power of collaboration.* Cambridge, MA: Basic Books.

Schein, E. 2008. Creating and managing culture: The essence of leadership. In *Business Leadership: A Jossey-Bass Reader*, 2nd ed., ed. J. Gallos, 362–369. San Francisco: John Wiley and Sons.

Wagner, T., and R. Kegan. 2006. *Change leadership: A practical guide to transforming our schools.* San Francisco: Jossey-Bass.

Wenger, E. n.d. Communities of practice: A brief introduction. *www.ewenger.com/theory/index.htm*

Wheatley, M. 2002. *Turning to one another: Simple conversations to restore hope to the future.* San Francisco: Berrett-Koehler.

Chapter 3

Teaching Learning Collaborative:

A Process for Supporting Professional Learning Communities[1]

Kathryn DiRanna, Jo Topps, Karen Cerwin, and Susan Gomez-Zwiep

"I used to think that I taught it; they just didn't learn it.
Now I know that I have a responsibility in orchestrating
student understanding. Working with my colleagues in this
learning community increases the effectiveness of my lesson
design, my teaching practice, and my student learning."

—Teacher participating in the Teaching Learning Collaborative

Chapter 3

Ask teachers to describe how they plan a lesson and their responses often focus on the following: looking at the standard they should be teaching, staying on target with the district's pacing guide, and identifying the activities they have in their instructional materials (or the file cabinet) and what science equipment is available. How students think or what they know about the concept to be taught is often absent from the conversation, as is the idea of using student work to guide instruction. Rarely do teachers describe collaborating with their colleagues in planning lessons, teaching, or reflecting on the effectiveness of the lesson on student learning.

Contrast that with teachers who have been a part of a particular type of professional learning community (PLC) called the Teaching Learning Collaborative (TLC). In this professional development strategy developed over the past 12 years by WestEd's K–12 Alliance, teachers working in collaborative teams design lessons for student learning. Based on data, and beginning with the end in mind, these teachers sequence specific questions and activities to link students' prior knowledge to the learning sequence concept(s). The TLC participants team-teach the lesson and analyze student work from the lesson to identify a range of student understanding of the concept. The teachers then use the data to monitor and adjust their instructional practices.

How Is the TLC a PLC?

A PLC in which teachers and administrators continuously seek and share learning and act on what they learn so that students benefit is a powerful staff development approach and a potent strategy for school change and improvement (Hord 1997). However, for PLCs to be effective, they must go beyond the platitudes of working collaboratively for the common good. They must provide structures and processes for the collaboration as well as for understanding the real work of teaching and learning. Without these structures and processes, PLCs run the risk of being another professional development "du jour" without any real impact on student learning, and with a real risk of increasing the attitude that "this too shall pass."

In developing the TLC, we recognized that there were many challenges to teachers working collaboratively—they may not have a history of doing so, they do not have time or a clear purpose for coming together, and they often lack the skills or the protocols to be successful as a collaborative group. We also recognized that teachers were isolated, often engaged in classroom management rather than focusing on student learning, and frequently ill-equipped to monitor teaching and learning in their classrooms. We wanted to change this paradigm by using the TLC as a structured way to focus teacher discourse and reflection and school action on student learning in science. We designed tools and processes to ensure that the TLC learning community stayed focused on specifying desired learning outcomes, planning quality science lessons, assessing student learning, and taking action when students did not learn.

1 The content of this chapter is based on the collaborative work of the K–12 Alliance at WestEd, which includes the authors and Cindy Anderson, Diane Carnahan, David Harris, Kathryn Schultz, Jody Sherriff, Greta Smith, Melissa Smith, and Rita Starnes.

The TLC design aligns with many of the characteristics of PLCs (DuFour et al. 2006; Hord 1997; Louis and Kruse 1995). In particular, the TLC process helps teachers *identify shared values and vision* about conceptual teaching, student-centered instruction, and quality student work for all students. Through *collaborative* planning, team-teaching, and debriefing the effectiveness of the learning sequence design, teachers *share their practice* and *engage in reflective dialogue*. The focus on what students should know and understand is measured by the *quality of student work* generated in the lesson. The entire process creates a culture of collaboration that is *supportive* and *self-sustaining*. As noted by a TLC teacher, "The TLC is a PLC!"

In this chapter we share the TLC processes and tools as an example of a PLC focused on the real work of teaching science in daily classroom practice. Through the use of a vignette we explicate how teachers work collaboratively to achieve their goals for student learning.

What Is a TLC?

The TLC is a unique professional development strategy that engages groups of teachers in collaborative planning and teaching of a science lesson, coaching and mentoring, and examining student work. The TLC design reflects research on professional development, including the importance of developing teachers' understanding of science content, providing teachers with opportunities for professional dialogue and critical reflection, and focusing closely on the classroom and the impact on student learning (Loucks-Horsley et al. 2003, Weiss et al. 1999; Cohen and Hill 1998).

The TLC was originally developed as a way for teams of teachers who attended science content institutes to apply their learning in the classroom. The TLC focuses on identifying specific content that students should know and understand, and designing a learning sequence that facilitates quality student thinking and work. Working in teams of four, teachers and a facilitator participate in an iterative process of making their lessons better and better (sometimes referred to as "polishing the stone") as they plan for student learning; analyze student work from the team-taught lesson; and redesign for student learning based on the data from the team-taught lesson (see Figure 3.1). TLC teams then repeat the sequence in another classroom.

Figure 3.1. Teaching Learning Collaborative Overview

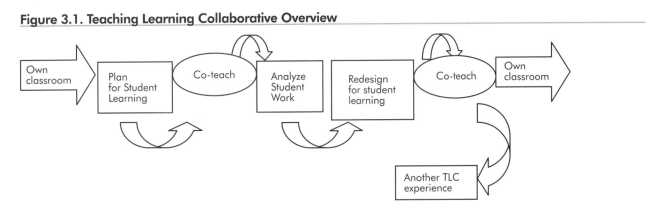

Chapter 3

The TLC sessions are most often conducted in two- to three-day sets, including a day of planning and a day or two of teaching and debriefing. TLC teams first *plan for student learning* by identifying a topic or concept to teach that is relevant to where their students are in the curriculum, and they select two similar classrooms in which to teach the lesson. The team designs a learning sequence, which is a series of activities/investigations that facilitate student understanding of a science concept. A learning sequence may be completed in one lesson (e.g., one hour) or may last several days. They then team-teach the learning sequence, with each person teaching a part—an excellent example of shared practice. This is followed by a debrief of the effectiveness of the lesson, where the team *analyzes student work* and transcriptions of teacher practice to determine whether the design of the learning sequence had an impact on student learning. The learning sequence is then *redesigned for student learning* based on evidence from the classroom and then taught to another group of students. The process of looking at student work is repeated and the learning sequence is refined for future use in other TLC experiences or in the teachers' individual classrooms.

Team Structure

The quality of discussion in a PLC depends on the development of supportive structures in which they take place (Graham 2007). The TLC teams are designed to accomplish many of the goals of a school-based PLC: diminish isolation, encourage collaboration, and enable professional discourse to blossom and flourish. Incentives to participate on a TLC team vary. Some teachers are motivated by extrinsic incentives such as stipends; other teachers are motivated as part of a school improvement plan or in response to test scores; and still others are motivated as part of their desire for continuous improvement.

TLC teams consist of four teachers; a process facilitator who coordinates and plans with the team, transcribes the actual teaching, and conducts the debriefs; and, if possible, a content expert (e.g., a university partner) who during planning helps the team focus on content questions and identify student misconceptions. Facilitators monitor and assist beginning teams; more experienced teams rotate the facilitator role among all participants, thus sharing leadership.

The composition of the teacher teams can be varied. We have had success with grade-level teams and with teams that cross grade levels, as well as with teams composed of veteran and new teachers. The makeup of the team is most often determined by the school site or district that is using the TLC strategy. Teams are formed based on a variety of contextual factors: discipline specificity (e.g., life, Earth, or physical science), teaching schedules, availability of release time for planning, and substitutes to cover the teaching day.

The efficacy of the teacher teams is important for collaborative work to be accomplished. Every effort is made to construct teams that are amicable and have the same goals; however, when that is not possible, the facilitator helps the group establish good working relations using strategies such as *ways of talking* and the *norms of collaboration* (Garmston and Wellman 2000). What matters to the success of the team are the qualities of openness, trust, mutual respect, supportive leadership, flexibility, and a willingness to embrace ambiguity. Once teams are established, they determine their planning-teaching-debriefing schedule based on their needs. For example, they may meet during a shared planning period, after school, or on a release day to plan or debrief the lesson.

The Power of Collaboration: A TLC Vignette

To understand the power of a TLC as a PLC, we use a vignette from a fourth-grade team; their story is woven throughout the chapter. The type of collaborative work, focus on student learning, and reflection on teacher practice that is demonstrated in the vignette is representative of TLCs from elementary, middle, and high school teams.

It is midmorning. The four fourth-grade teachers have just team-taught their initial learning sequence that they designed earlier in the week with their facilitator. The focus of the lesson was on complete electric circuits, a concept identified through the conceptual flow process explained in the section "Identifying a Learning Sequence Concept" later in this chapter. During the planning, most of the teachers said that they had taught a "make it light" activity with their students the year before. Based on that teaching experience, they were sure that students would understand the idea that electricity flows in a complete circuit and that connections between batteries, bulbs, and wires are needed to make the bulb light.

During the team-teaching of the lesson, the facilitator documented the learning sequence by transcribing teacher and student dialogue, as well as noting student engagement and actions. Having team-taught the lesson, it was now time to debrief. With the facilitator, the team reviewed her transcription of the lesson and analyzed trends in what the students wrote in their science notebooks in answer to the prompt shown in Figure 3.2.

In planning the lesson, the team thought about what students would say in response to the prompt. The team had expected the students to

Figure 3.2. Student Prompt

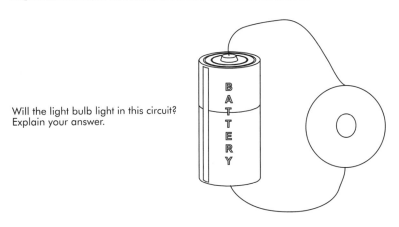

Will the light bulb light in this circuit? Explain your answer.

BATTERY

write statements such as "It will light because it is a complete circuit"; "It will work because the electricity will flow in a path"; "It will light because the battery, bulb, and wires are connected to make a complete path or circuit." However, when the team examined the student work, analyzed the data, and looked for patterns and trends in student thinking, they were surprised to find that only two students used the academic vocabulary of a complete circuit and only four expressed the idea that "parts" needed to be connected. Five students said the electricity works because it goes in a circle. Seven students mentioned "parts" of the circuit rather than being specific about the battery, bulb, and wires. Five students repeated the prompt as their answer (i.e., "It will work because it will work").

The characteristics in the student work (e.g., "circle" meaning circuit; using "parts" rather than stating the specific part; no mention of anything being connected) caused the teachers to reflect on their instructional design for the student exploration with circuits. The team realized that they had given directions for the exploration but had not designed specific questions to probe student thinking as they were exploring the circuits. As part of the redesign for learning, the teachers crafted clarifying and probing questions they thought would deepen student thinking during the exploration when they taught the lesson again.

Components of a TLC/PLC: Focus on Student Learning

The teachers had focused carefully on students' answers and were reflective about what teacher "moves" would elicit deeper understanding. How did this PLC, based on a collaborative culture, come to these realizations? To answer this question, we need to retrace their steps in planning and delivering this learning sequence concept.

> As one TLC participant noted, "This experience proves [to me] the effectiveness of collaboration in teaching. When strong educational professionals put their minds together, the product becomes a tool for the advancement of student understanding. I look forward to finishing the lesson tomorrow and using the same techniques and methods in future lessons. AWESOME!"

The four teachers who were engaged in the TLC process focused on the design of instructional sequences that maximize student learning. This process reflects DuFour's guiding questions for PLCs (DuFour 2004; DuFour et al. 2006):

- What do we want students to learn?
- How will we know when they have learned it?
- What do we do when students experience difficulty?

The three TLC steps that mirror DuFour's guiding questions for clarifying student learning outcomes, assessing students' learning, and making adjustments to ensure learning are

- plan for student learning,
- analyze student work, and
- redesign for student learning.

Plan for Student Learning

All TLC participants engage in a science content institute in which they learn the processes of planning a learning sequence, including (1) identifying a learning goal (learning sequence concept); (2) designing a learning sequence that moves students from their prior knowledge toward the learning sequence concept; and (3) developing questions that elicit a full range of student understanding. Each of these is briefly described in the following sections.

Identifying a Learning Sequence Concept

The teachers begin the learning sequence design by beginning with the end in mind. They develop a *conceptual flow* (DiRanna 1989; DiRanna and Topps 2004; DiRanna et al. 2008) that links the big ideas or concepts that teachers think are important for students to know, the standards teachers are responsible for teaching, and the content presented in the instructional materials. The conceptual flow differs from a concept map in that the flow addresses concepts in a unit of instruction (in the case of a TLC, it addresses the concepts in a lesson) and has both a hierarchy of ideas (indicating the relationship between and among the ideas) and a direction (i.e., the sequence for instruction).

Constructing a conceptual flow provides teachers with a springboard for establishing shared norms and values through conversations about student learning (e.g., they identify important concepts for learning and assessment for which resources such as the *Atlas of Science Literacy* [AAAS 2001, 2007] can be referenced) and teacher practice (e.g., they identify an instructional sequence for which resources [textbooks, instructional materials] can be used to support learning). Laying this foundation is critical to determining the sequence of instruction. As one TLC participant noted, "[Developing the conceptual flow] moved us from a list of topics to...nesting of important ideas. Identifying what really matters for student understanding drives decisions about...questions in instruction and assessment."

The fourth-grade team in the vignette began the development of their conceptual flow by identifying what topic they would teach: complete electric circuits. They then explored the prompt "What should an exiting fourth-grade student know about complete circuits?" With the guidance of the facilitator, the teachers each wrote a complete paragraph that described the concepts, or big ideas, that students should know. Through a guided activity, teachers rewrote the concepts/ big ideas on different-size sticky notes. The size of the sticky note corresponded to the size of the idea—bigger ideas on larger notes, smaller ideas on smaller notes.

The teachers used their sticky notes to position how the concepts and ideas fit together and designed a conceptual flow that represented a synthesis of their thinking. Figure 3.3 illustrates the team's conceptual flow for electric circuits. Through this process, the team addressed the question "What do we want students to learn?"; they collaboratively identified a clear concept on which to base their lesson, and they developed a common vision about where the concept of circuits fits into the larger topic of electricity.

Figure 3.3. Fourth-Grade Team Conceptual Flow

Electricity flows in a complete circuit.

A complete circuit allows the flow of electricity when its components (e.g., battery, bulb, and wires) are connected to form a complete path.

Complete circuits can be series or parallel.

Electricity in circuits can produce light, heat, sound, and magnetic effects.

A switch is a device that opens or closes a complete circuit.

Materials that allow the flow of electricity are called conductors.

Materials that do not allow the flow of electricity are called insulators.

The team determined which of the big ideas would be selected as the learning sequence concept: "A complete circuit allows the flow of electricity when its components (e.g., battery, bulb, and wires) are connected to form a complete path." This is indicated in the gray box in Figure 3.3.

Designing a Learning Sequence

The TLC process helps teachers clarify what they want students to learn by designing a learning sequence that incorporates student-centered experiences to move students from their prior knowledge toward the learning goal. In order to do this, teams use a modified version of Bybee's (1997) 5E instructional model (i.e., engage, explore, explain, elaborate, and evaluate). The TLC modified this model to focus the elaborate stage on extending the understanding of the learning sequence concept, and the evaluate stage is focused on decision point assessments throughout the sequence (see DPA in Figure 3.4). The TLC process also adds a concept column for each stage to link student prior knowledge to the learning goal. TLC teams use the template illustrated in Figure 3.4 to collaboratively develop the learning sequence.

Figure 3.4. 5E Learning Sequence Planning Template

Learning Sequence Concept_____

Teacher Does	Student Does	Concept
ENGAGE Questions/Prompts/Activities	(student thinking) Expected Student Responses	Engage Concept(s)
——— DPA ———		
EXPLORE Questions/Prompts/Activities	(student thinking) Expected Student Responses	Explore Concept(s)
——— DPA ———		
EXPLAIN Questions/Prompts/Activities	(student thinking) Expected Student Responses	Learning Sequence Concept
——— DPA ———		
EXTEND Questions/Prompts/Activities	(student thinking) Expected Student Responses	Extend Concept
——— DPA ———		

Note: DPA = decision point assessment

By using this template, teachers identify concepts and student thinking before selecting instructional activities. It's important to be clear on what we want students to get out of the lesson. We need to ask questions to help students see relationships and make connections.

The fourth-grade team in the vignette used this template to plan for the initial teaching experience. The TLC processes helped them embrace the tenets of a PLC: Teachers shared ideas from their current teaching practices, struggled with and clarified their understanding of the content they were to teach, and reflected on the best questions and sequence of activities to elicit student learning.

The team began their planning in the Concept column with the end in mind—what they wanted their students to learn. In other words, what is/are the concept(s) that students should be able to explain if they understand the learning sequence concept (DuFour et al. 2006)? As noted earlier, the fourth-grade team identified the concept that "a complete circuit allows the flow of electricity when its components (e.g., battery, bulb, and wires) are connected to form a complete path."

The team then considered what prior knowledge students should have and discussed what concepts students would need to explore in order to fully understand the learning sequence concept. In their plan, the teachers identified "batteries are a power source" as the prior knowledge concept and "electric circuits have parts that when connected in a complete path will light the bulb" as the primary concept that students would investigate in the explore stage.

With the Concept column completed, the team was able to focus on the question "How will we know that the students understand?" The team accomplished this by planning for the Student Does column. The teachers predicted what the students would think, say, and do as a result of instructional activities. Predicting expected student responses (ESRs) enables teachers to draft initial questions and follow-up prompts that elicit the full range of student understanding. Finally, the team thought about the questions, prompts, and activities that would elicit the learning and added them to the Teacher Does column. In Table 3.1, note the planned coherence of each stage from teacher question/activity to ESR to address the concept.

Developing Questions That Elicit a Full Range of Student Understanding

The effectiveness of the learning sequence depends on having students engage in authentic work that challenges their thinking and provides opportunities for them to demonstrate their understanding of content. We believe that this type of student work results from asking appropriate questions to elicit student understanding and promoting student-to-student discourse to refine and extend student understanding.

Good questioning requires skill and planning (Kruger and Sutton 2001) to get beyond the typical low-level yes/no, recall, rhetorical, and leading questions. Through the TLC process teachers recognize that they have to ask quality questions that

Table 3.1. 5E Learning Sequence: Initial Lesson

Learning Sequence Concept: Electricity flows in a complete circuit (a complete circuit allows the flow of electricity when its components, e.g., battery, bulb, and wires, are connected to form a complete path).

5E	Teacher Does	Student Does	Concept
Engage	(Teacher displays a variety of battery-powered toys.) Let's think about how these toys work. Talk to your elbow partner about how the toys work. (Think-pair-share) What makes them work? What do the batteries do? What happens when we take the battery out of the toy?	Students talk to their elbow partner. Batteries make them work. Batteries make them go. The battery charge. The switch. Remote control. Power. Electricity. Makes it go. Gives it energy. Gives the power. It doesn't work. It's dead. It's broken. You have to get new batteries.	Batteries are one part of the circuit found in battery-powered toys.
Explore	Let's explore batteries, bulbs, and wires when they are not in a toy to see how they work. Your job is to find a way to make the bulb light using a battery and wires. Once you get the bulb to light, draw a picture of your connections in your science notebook. Label connections as complete circuits.	Students try many combinations to make the bulb light until they are successful. Students draw connections in their science notebooks.	Electric circuits have parts that can be connected. When the parts are connected in a complete path the bulb will light.
Explain	Take a look at the circuit I drew on the board. Will the light bulb light in this circuit? Explain your answer. Write your answer in your science journal.	It will light because the battery, bulb and wires are connected to make a complete path or circuit. It will work because it is a complete circuit. It will work because the electricity will flow in a path.	A complete circuit allows the flow of electricity when its components, e.g., battery, bulb, and wires, are connected to form a complete path.
Extend	NOT CONSIDERED AS PART OF THIS LEARNING SEQUENCE DESIGN AT THIS POINT		

continue with the student's line of reasoning, pushing and probing for underlying assumptions, alternate conceptions, and partial understanding. Crafting probing questions and predicting ESRs addresses one of DuFour et al.'s (2006) questions for PLCs, What do we do when students experience difficulty? Predicting ESRs helps teachers be prepared. It enables the teachers to share their prior experiences with teaching the specific content and to identify the common student answers/misconceptions that need to be addressed. It helps teachers think about connecting with what students do know. When students verbalize what the teachers have expected (including misconceptions), the teacher can more easily probe or clarify student thinking and keep students from experiencing difficulty. As one TLC participant stated, "Students think differently and we don't always anticipate their responses. Jointly planning questions and possible student responses in the TLC teaches us how to pre-think what students will say so that we can be prepared. It is much better than being caught off guard and having to think on our feet as to where this student is going."

Note in the initial lesson (see Table 3.1) that the questions listed under what the teacher does are mostly directional prompts. After teaching and debriefing the lesson and analyzing student work, the team realized that they had not designed many questions to probe student thinking during the exploration. The teachers refined the questions (see the section "Redesign for Student Learning" later in this chapter) based on actual student responses in the first lesson.

Analyze Student Work

PLCs are grounded in the examination of student data and the use of that data to improve instruction and student learning. In the TLC process, analyzing student work is a major construct of helping teachers shift their paradigm from a focus on teaching to a focus on learning. The team uses two structured debriefs (one after the team has team-taught the initial lesson; the second on the same day after the team has team-taught the redesigned lesson) to call attention to the effectiveness of their design for learning and to modify or redesign the learning sequence to increase student understanding.

During each debrief, the team uses two sources to examine the effectiveness of the learning sequence design: the facilitator's transcription and the student work. Team members comment on the parts of the lesson they thought were effective or not effective and provide specific evidence to support their comments. The team looks at the lesson transcript and student work to validate or refute their claims and to determine which parts of the learning sequence need to be redesigned to increase student understanding.

In the first debrief (after teaching the initial learning sequence), participants use a "quick sort" to see how the students are responding to the prompts. In the second debrief (after teaching the redesigned learning sequence), team members build on their ideas about student responses and the characteristics in student work to develop a scoring rubric.

When the fourth-grade team in the vignette began their first debrief, they reviewed their ESRs for the student work. They quickly sorted the student papers into piles of high-, medium-, and low-level responses; discussed the characteristics of each pile; and noted any general trends in the work. As described earlier, they had expected students to understand and express what a complete circuit was, but the student work was lacking in several areas. The learning sequence needed to be redesigned to elicit better student work.

Redesign for Student Learning

A goal of the TLC process, like a PLC, is to provide quality learning for all students. In the case of the TLC this means not only paying attention to the number of students engaged in the lesson but also providing multiple opportunities to move students from where they are conceptually to an understanding of the learning sequence concept. To this end, TLC teams use the data from the student work as the basis for the redesign of the learning sequence. The team reviews prompts and ESRs and decides which parts of the sequence to keep, which parts need to be modified, and which parts need to be deleted or added in order to enhance student learning of the concept.

In the vignette, the fourth-grade team decided to make three modifications to the learning sequence:

1. the addition of more strategic questions to probe student understanding;
2. the addition of another explore activity in which students would use *think alouds* (a strategy where students verbalize what they are thinking as they explore) as a scaffold for expressing the concept in words and drawing a complete circuit on a group-size whiteboard for small-group discussion and on the class whiteboard for large-group discussion; and
3. a new "explain" prompt for students to explain their understanding. The student work generated from this prompt would be evaluated for the effectiveness of the redesign for student learning.

Strategic Questions

The team realized that the questions in the initial lesson were actually prompts for directions. None of the questions were designed to probe for student understanding. Thus, the team redesigned the questions based on the student responses from the initial lesson, to help students clarify the parts of the circuit and the connections necessary for a complete circuit and to redirect student thinking that circuits had to be circles. Figure 3.5 is a transcript of the redesigned teacher questions and the resulting student responses.

Figure 3.5. Transcript of Redesigned Teacher Questions and Student Responses

Teacher (T): *Why did the lightbulb light?*
Student 1 (S1): *Because it is a complete circuit.*

T: (clarify) *Explain what you mean by a complete circuit.*
S1: *It is when electricity goes in a circle.*

T: (reflect) *Does it have to be a circle? Could it be another shape?*
Student 2 (S2): *Yes, it is always a circle.*

T: (redirect) *What would happen if we placed the parts in a square? Would it be possible for the bulb to light?*
S2: Student hesitates…then says…*Yes, the bulb could light in a square.*

T: (probe) *Can you think of another shape for the complete circuit in addition to a circle or a square?*
S1: *A triangle could also be the shape for the circuit.*

T: (clarify) *You've told me it would work in a circle, in a square, and in a triangle. What parts do they have in common?*
S1: *A battery, a wire, and a bulb.*

T: (clarify) *How do the parts help make the lightbulb light?*
S1: *One wire needs to touch the metal part on the bottom of the lightbulb and one end of the battery, and one wire needs to touch the metal on the side of the lightbulb and the other side of the battery.*

T: (summarize) *How would you add this information to your idea of a complete circuit?*
S1: *So parts need to be connected in a complete circuit.*

The team would discuss this transcript during the debrief of the second lesson. (See the section "Analysis of Student Work One More Time" later in this chapter.)

The team also thought it was important to have students draw a complete circuit in their notebook as well as a drawing of a circuit that did not work. The team decided that having students draw both types of circuits and discussing the differences between them would help the students understand better the connections that are required for a circuit to be complete. Additionally, the team decided to ask students to label the connections that worked as complete circuits.

Think Aloud Explore Activity

The second modification to the learning sequence, the think aloud activity, was added as a result of the team's realization that only a few of the students were correctly describing a complete circuit and the connectedness of the pathway. The teachers wanted to ensure that all students could demonstrate this understanding. Two of the teachers on the team were concerned that students were not considering the filament as part of the pathway.

In the new explore activity (see Table 3.2), students would come to the front board and draw a picture of a complete circuit that will light the bulb and one that does not, and then the class would discuss the differences. By first having the whole class "think aloud," the team anticipated that all students would see the difference between circuits that light the bulb and those that do not. By also having students, in small groups, draw their circuit on the group whiteboard, teachers could quickly check that all students were contributing to the drawing and that all students could physically trace the flow of electricity in their pathway. If the teachers noticed that no filaments were drawn in the bulb, teachers could probe student thinking as to how the electricity got through the lightbulb.

Table 3.2. Additional Explore Stage of 5E Learning Sequence With a Whiteboard Experience

Stage	Teacher Does	Student Does	Concept
Explore	Ask a student to come to the board and draw one way the bulb will light. Ask the student to "think aloud" as he/she draws. Ask another student to come to the board and draw one way the bulb will not light.	Students use the drawings from their notebook.	Electric circuits have parts that can be connected. When the parts are connected in a complete path, the bulb will light.
	Ask the class, What is different about the two drawings? What is the same? What is needed for the lightbulb to light?	Things that are the same are battery, bulb, and wires. What is different is that in the bulb that lights, all things are connected in a complete path.	
	Now I would like groups to draw a picture of a complete circuit on their whiteboard.	Students use the drawings in their science notebooks to draw a larger image of the complete circuit on the whiteboard.	
	Make sure that student drawings include all parts of the complete circuit.		
	I would like you to use your finger to trace the path of the electricity on your drawing.	Students trace the path of the electricity.	
	If students do not include the filament in their drawing, have students look more closely to examine the inside of the lightbulb. Have students add the filament to their drawing.		
	Make sure that all students have included the filament in their drawings.	Students include filament.	
	I would like you to use your finger to trace the path of the electricity on your drawing. Be sure to include the filament.	Students trace the path of the electricity through the filament.	

New Explain Prompt
With the redesign of the learning sequence, the team decided to change the explain stage to build on what students experienced in the explore stage. They constructed a prompt (see Table 3.3) that expanded their original concept to now include the filament in completing the circuit.

Table 3.3. New Explain Stage of 5E Learning Sequence

Stage	Teacher Does	Student Does	Concept
Explain	Take a look at the circuit on your worksheet. Will this lightbulb work? Tell me why or why not.	The lightbulb will not work. The circuit has a battery, bulb, and wire. It is not a complete circuit because the filament is broken/missing. The path for the flow of electricity is not connected.	A complete circuit allows the flow of electricity when its components (e.g., battery, bulb [including filament], and wires) are connected to form a complete path.

With the redesign complete (usually within an hour), the team is ready to re-teach the new sequence to a new set of students. Once again the teachers team-teach and the facilitator transcribes the teacher and student talk.

Analysis of Student Work One More Time

After teaching the second time, the team is ready to debrief, using both the facilitator's transcript and student work and responses to analyze the effectiveness of the redesigned learning sequence. From the transcript in the vignette (see Figure 3.5), the fourth-grade teachers agreed that by building on what students might say (based on student work from the first lesson) and planning questions to probe for student learning, they were able to help students clarify their ideas about circuits. The teachers discussed ways in which the revised questioning sequence resulted in changes in student thinking:

- It helped students move away from their initial idea that a circuit is a circle.
- It encouraged students to recognize and label the common parts in these circuits (battery, bulb, wires).
- It reinforced students' understanding that everything is connected in a complete circuit.

Next, the team reviewed the groups' whiteboards. They noted that most groups had drawn complete circuits, labeled the components, and included the filament.

Finally, the team analyzed the student work from the "explain prompt." The team used a process of rubric development that evolved from the ESRs (DiRanna et al. 2008). The team expected students to explain that the bulb will not light because the filament is broken or missing and that it, too, is a part of the complete circuit. The facilitator asked the team to take a look at the student work gathered from the lesson and separate it into three piles: high-, medium-, and low-level responses. This was followed by a discussion of the characteristics and specific information within each of the three performance levels, which the team used to develop a scoring rubric that included qualitative descriptors of student work.

Table 3.4 illustrates the transition from expected student responses to a scoring rubric. In the first row are the ESRs from the redesigned learning sequence before it is taught. Note that the team only recorded high and low ESRs. In the second row, the facilitator asked the team to take a look at the student work gathered from the lesson and separate it into three piles: high-, medium-, and low-level responses. This was followed by a discussion of characteristics of high-, medium-, and low-level performance and recorded on the chart (Table 3.4). The team then generalized from the characteristics to make the scoring rubric on the third row. The initial

ESRs represent the teacher expectations; the final rubric is a modification based on student work. In this example, in addition to adding descriptive qualities to the rubric, the teachers also changed the low-level response from expecting students to not answer the prompt to answering correctly with limited descriptions.

Table 3.4. Characteristics of Low-, Medium-, and High-Level Responses

Source	Low-Level Response	Medium-Level Response	High-Level Response
Expected student response from redesigned lesson sequence	Will not flow, with no explanation.		Electricity from the battery will not flow through the wires and lightbulb because the filament is not connected and the circuit is not complete.
Characteristics from looking at student work	Says it won't work. Doesn't use the word *filament*.	Mentions some but not all parts (but does say something about the filament). Says it won't work.	Has all the parts. Says it won't work because it is not a complete connection. Uses the word *circuit*.
Scoring rubric	Answers correctly. States that something is missing in the lightbulb or circuit. Does not mention the word *filament*. Mentions that electricity is needed.	Answers correctly. May mention one or more parts of the circuit, including filament. Mentions connections needed for a complete flow of electricity. May use the words *complete path* or *circuit*.	Answers correctly. Clearly states that the complete circuit has a battery, bulb, wire, and filament connected in a path for the electricity to flow. Uses the words *complete path* or *circuit*.

The team used the scoring rubric to look at patterns and trends in the student work. The data provided evidence that the modifications they made in the redesign of the learning sequence were effective. More students used academic vocabulary and indicated an understanding of a complete circuit, including the filament. Based on this analysis, the team discussed interventions for each student as well as interventions for the class in the next lesson.

It is now late afternoon. The fourth-grade team and facilitator have collaboratively planned, taught, and debriefed two lessons focusing on the interaction of teaching and learning. Their reflections centered on how to design for student learning by carefully crafting questions and activities based on ESRs, actual student work, and rubrics that provide constructive feedback to students to improve the quality of their work.

This PLC of teachers will repeat the TLC experience three to nine times during a school year. With each experience, teams mature as professionals, de-privatizing their practice, negotiating and constructing a common understanding of the content they teach, identifying their expectations for student performance, and identifying the methods necessary for evaluating the effectiveness of their teaching.

Chapter 3

By systematically working together, the teams are strengthening their professional knowledge and building a common vision around student learning—shifting their focus from teaching to ensuring learning for all.

Reflection Questions

- What structures exist within your context that support the implementation of a TLC? Which structures might inhibit the use of this model?
- To what extent does your current culture support collaboration? To what extent does your current culture provide avenues to support a TLC-like process? What cultural features would need to be added or modified?
- How are lesson study strategies being used in your context? What can you extract from this chapter that would assist you in enhancing or developing and implementing a lesson study design similar to the TLC process?

References

American Association for the Advancement of Science (AAAS). 2001. *Atlas of science literacy.* Vol. 1. Washington, DC: AAAS.

American Association for the Advancement of Science (AAAS). 2007. *Atlas of science literacy.* Vol. 2. Washington, DC: AAAS.

Bybee, R. W. 1997. *Achieving scientific literacy: From purposes to practices.* Portsmouth, NH: Heinemann.

Cohen, D., and H. Hill. 1998. *Instructional policy and classroom performance: The mathematics reform in California.* RR-39. Philadelphia: Consortium for Policy and Research in Education, 1998.

DiRanna, K., ed. 1989. *What's the big idea training manual.* Irvine, CA: California Science Implementation Network.

DiRanna, K., and J. Topps. 2004. *Going with the flow. What's the big idea?* Santa Ana, CA: K–12 Alliance/WestEd.

DiRanna, K., E. Osmundson, J. Topps, L. Barakos, M. Gearhart, K. Cerwin, D. Carnahan, and C. Strang. 2008. *Assessment-centered teaching: A reflective practice.* Thousand Oaks, CA: Corwin Press.

DuFour, R. 2004. What is a "professional learning community?" *Educational Leadership* 61 (8): 6–11.

DuFour, R., R. DuFour, R. Eaker, and T. Many. 2006. *Learning by doing: A handbook for professional learning communities at work.* Bloomington, IN: Solution Tree.

Garmston, R., and B. Wellman. 2000. *The adaptive school: Developing and facilitating collaborative groups.* El Dorado Hills, CA: Four Hats Seminars.

Graham, P. 2007. The role of conversation, contention, and commitment in a professional learning community. *Connexions* module m14270. *http://cnx.org/content/m14270/latest/*

Hord, S. M. 1997. *Professional learning communities: Communities of continuous inquiry and improvement.* Austin, TX: Southwest Educational Development Laboratory. Available at: *www.sedl.org/pubs/catalog/items/cha34.html*

Kruger, A., and J. Sutton, eds. 2001. *Ed thoughts: What we know about science teaching and learning.* Aurora, CO: Mid-continent Research for Education and Learning (McREL).

Loucks-Horsley, S., N. Love, K. E. Stiles, S. Mundry, and P. Hewson. 2003. *Designing professional development for teachers of science and mathematics.* 2nd ed. Thousand Oaks, CA: Corwin Press.

Louis, K. S., and S. D. Kruse, eds. 1995. *Professionalism and community.* Thousand Oaks, CA: Corwin Press.

Weiss, I. R., G. B. Gellatly, D. L. Montgomery, C. J. Ridgway, C. D. Templeton, and D. Whittington. 1999. *Executive summary of the local systemic change through teacher enhancement year four cross-site report.* Chapel Hill, NC: Horizon Research Inc.

Chapter 4

Building Professional Development Cadres

Hedi Baxter Lauffer and Dan Lauffer

"If you want to build a ship, don't herd people together
to collect wood and don't assign them tasks and work,
but rather teach them to long for the
endless immensity of the sea."

—Antoine de Saint-Exupéry, *The Wisdom of the Sands*

Chapter 4

We begin with a vignette based on several anecdotes told to us during our years working in the Los Angeles basin with a cadre of professional developers. This story sets the stage for exploring challenges tackled by our K–16 professional learning community (PLC).

Maria's teacher, Ms. Wake, is in her second year of teaching, and it may be her last. Ms. Wake was excited to start teaching her first year when she was assigned to teach eighth-grade science, but it just hasn't worked out the way she imagined. It was hard. She didn't feel very well prepared to teach the subject or manage her classes. Ms. Wake took an interesting biology course at the state university where she earned certification, but the notes she took from that lecture didn't look like the eighth-grade science standards. She also had an education methods course that included two weeks on teaching science, but that became mostly a blur once the school year began.

During this first month of school, Ms. Wake is to teach students about density and buoyancy. She is not sure if she understands what density really is, and she knows even less about buoyancy. Last year she had students memorize formulas and practice using them. Several times her class erupted into a fight when her back was turned, and students complained a lot about being bored or not understanding. Ms. Wake attended a three-day workshop for middle school science teachers last year, and she met a lot of other teachers who were struggling, too. The workshop organizer was new to his position as a science leader, and he talked about what he did in his classroom, but Ms. Wake felt her students were very different. Workshop participants practiced asking questions as part of a discussion about science inquiry, but they seemed like questions she couldn't imagine her students asking.

Ms. Wake has a few new activities to try this year, but she is also looking for a different job. Maria and some of her classmates may learn enough facts from Ms. Wake's class to score proficiently on the state test, but they have little chance of getting to conceptual understanding of density, buoyancy, or the other eighth-grade science standards.

Ms. Wake's vignette is filled with well-meaning educators and deserving students, but it does not culminate in a vision for science teaching and learning that we can celebrate. The education system in this all-too-common scenario is an ineffective network. Ms. Wake did not simply slip through the cracks of an otherwise solid program; the system failed to prepare and support her. With the large number of middle school teachers and high turnover rate typical to urban districts, we simply cannot afford to put teachers like Ms. Wake through a disconnected series of preservice college courses and district professional development and hope for the best. Nor can we ignore the need to effectively support university faculty and professional developers to do a better job preparing and supporting teachers.

The essential question is, how can we effectively engage preservice and inservice teachers in professional learning that is coherent and aligned to a shared vision for science teaching and learning? What we address in this chapter is the way a PLC evolved to address that problem over five years' work in the Los Angeles basin. Our work was funded by a National Science Foundation project called System-wide Change for All Learners and Educators (SCALE) and its sister project, Quality Educator Development (QED) math and science reform initiative, funded by the U.S. Department of Education.

Using both curriculum and professional development strategies to reform K–16 classroom practices, our project grew to build a PLC among district and university science educators to promote their professional learning as an essential element for taking science education improvement to scale in a large district. The science educators with whom we built this learning community were those district educators who provide professional development for their teacher-colleagues and the university faculty who work directly with teachers in science and education courses and outreach. In other words, we did not work directly with teachers (unless they also had responsibilities as professional developers) or specifically target administrators who were removed from working directly with teachers; rather, we worked with the *middle-level* science educators (not to be confused with middle school teachers).

Our focus on these middle-level educators draws on the strengths of those educators who have widespread and direct impact on classrooms. Rather than seeking a solution through a top-down reform approach, we adopted this "middle-out" PLC approach, because we believe that the people who directly interface with the challenges like those described in the story of Ms. Wake and Maria are the people best able to co-develop the solution. Therefore, what we share here is the story of a PLC composed of district science leaders, university science faculty, and education faculty in the Los Angeles basin who work primarily with Los Angeles Unified School District (LAUSD) teachers (Clifford and Millar 2007). These are individuals from different institutes of learning in the same region who are united by a commitment to their own learning and to collaborating to improve science education for all children and educators. From our experiences, we propose thinking beyond just using PLCs for teachers to improve student learning. SCALE shows us the value in establishing PLCs for professional development providers to improve teacher learning and build system-wide coherence.

Characteristics of the Professional Development Studygroup

Our work with the Professional Development Studygroup began with *science immersion*, an inquiry replacement unit approach to improving science teaching and learning in LAUSD and other SCALE districts. Although originally a minor part of the SCALE project, science immersion evolved into a significant strategy for cross-institutional systemic reform, with strong potential for sustainability in one of our nation's most challenging educational settings. Science immersion became a central focus of the work in the Los Angeles basin, and it has made a lasting impact on science education by shaping a common vision held by faculty, district practitioners, and teachers. This came about through the formation and work of a PLC that began with approximately 25 secondary LAUSD science leaders, eight California State University (CSU) education and science faculty, and several SCALE University of Wisconsin (UW) outreach educators. In February 2006, this community of learners (later named the Professional Development Studygroup) began convening monthly as a strategy for building the capacity to support preservice and inservice teachers to put into practice inquiry-based science learning for all LAUSD students. Figure 4.1 shows two PowerPoint slides used during the opening of each month's session; they are included here to illustrate the expectations and philosophy that guided the Studygroup's work.

Figure 4.1. PowerPoint Presentation of Professional Development (PD) Studygroup Participant Expectations and Philosophy

What is the philosophy that underpins *the Work*?

- *The Work* is guided, informed, and adjusted by evidence about what is best for supporting learners to learn

- All learners deserve an opportunity to develop deep conceptual understanding of science content by engaging in scientific habits of thinking

- Focused K-16 collaborative processes are valuable professional learning opportunities for science educators
    Building cross-institutional professional science education communities that can effectively support pre- and in-service teachers

What am I expected to do for this Work?

- Actively engage in all planning sessions
- Work collaboratively and according to agreed-upon norms
- Be open to new ideas; recognize the value in collaboration
- Share and increase our knowledge about relevant research and practices
- Co-facilitate sessions during summer teacher institutes and associated PD
- Be an expert and resource person for your unit
- Be a proponent for both Immersion Units and the processes of the PD Studygroup work

As shown in both the philosophy and expectations, the Professional Development Studygroup was a PLC with far greater goals than a train-the-trainer model for building capacity. Rather, the Studygroup served as a place for intellectual growth among colleagues working in different spheres of the same overall education system. It grew to become a K–16 group in 2007, and its members voted with their feet, attending with extraordinary regularity. LAUSD and CSU leadership recruited learning community members (middle-level educators), and those who agreed to join committed to the following:

- four two-day springtime professional development sessions in which learning to co-facilitate summer institutes for Science Immersion Units was the primary focus;
- at least one week in the summer co-facilitating a Science Immersion Institute; and
- three two-day sessions in the fall, building and reflecting on the Studygroup's prior work.

In compensation for Studygroup participation and associated co-facilitation work that took place outside of normal workdays, members received payment of the typical National Science Foundation stipend amount commensurate with their position.

Professional Development Studygroup meetings were consistently co-facilitated by the two lead SCALE science immersion outreach professionals. The goal was to build and sustain capacity to implement a coherent model of teacher professional development for the district and close-proximity state universities. While many PLCs focus solely on improving student learning, ours focused on developing coherence throughout the preservice and inservice teacher education system so that teachers like Ms. Wake and in fact all teachers would be effectively supported.

Additional co-facilitators for the Studygroup included both outside consultants and other SCALE staff who enriched meetings with their expertise and contributed individual facilitation for grade-level teams.

Typically, at least half of each two-day spring Studygroup meeting involved whole-group learning experiences, and the other half was reserved for grade-level team preparations. Figure 4.2 outlines the expected outcomes for the first session of the Studygroup, and Figure 4.3 summarizes the yearlong Studygroup activities.

Each of seven Professional Development Studygroup co-facilitation teams spent approximately 125 hours over the year in preparation for, and then reflecting on, the summer institutes and their own learning. The commitment of human and financial resources to this cross-institutional PLC was significant, but not extraordinary, and the effects were profound. Studygroup members reported feeling energized and revitalized, in addition to changing their practices.

Chapter 4

Figure 4.2. Expected Outcomes for Session 1 of Professional Development (PD) Studygroup

Session 1 Outcomes: As a result of participating in this professional development, participants will

- recognize how the SCALE Immersion Model for Professional Learning (SIMPL) supports learning effectively in multiple domains;
- develop an overall understanding of the significance for learners and teachers that the Engage-Explore-Explain paradigm plays in Immersion Units, and understand a strategy for making that visible to others;
- continue to develop and refine an understanding of the role that inquiry-based teaching and learning (as defined by the *National Science Education Standards*) plays in Immersion; and,
- develop an awareness of how Science Immersion PD Facilitation Guides are designed, developed, written, and revised to support science teaching and learning.

Figure 4.3. Overview of Outcomes for Professional Development (PD) Studygroup Sessions 2–7 and Associated Teacher PD Opportunities

Session 2: Continue to develop an understanding of and the ability to use the Professional Development framework and SIMPL for planning and facilitating effective sessions in the summer institutes and beyond. Practice facilitation during the first day.

Session 3: Working groups continue to plan summer institutes using the framework (from Session 2) and to revise specific agendas and facilitator guides for the institute sessions based on the previously agreed upon intended outcomes.

Session 4: Practice facilitation of the sessions with technical assistance and facilitated feedback. Work on co-facilitation strategies, skills, and agreements.

June, July, August: one-week Summer Science Immersion Institutes co-facilitated by PD Studygroup

October, December: half-day follow-up sessions for institute participants co-facilitated by PD Studygroup

Session 5: Reflect on the summer institute experiences and review participants' evaluations. Begin revisions to the follow-up PD sessions' facilitation guides.

Session 6: Reflect on our own practice in a Professional Development session study, using a version of the Tuning Protocol (adapted from the *Coalition of Essential Schools*). Prepare for and facilitate the follow-up agendas.

Session 7: Analyze and discuss feedback from classroom observations and the follow-up sessions. Transfer lessons learned to an intervention designed to support a different science education innovation from Immersion Units.

What set this program apart from other programs, which might also involve providing teacher institutes, was the approach to building a strong cadre of professional development providers and how we incorporated and attended to the tenets of a PLC. Hord and Sommers (2008, p. 9) identify five components of PLCs in *Leading Professional Learning Communities*:

1. shared beliefs, values, and vision;
2. shared and supportive leadership;
3. collective learning and its application;
4. supportive conditions; and
5. shared personal practice.

An endeavor such as the Professional Development Studygroup involves a complex interaction of strengths and challenges as it seeks to build an effectively functioning professional community. Deliberate and flexible planning is essential when developing a PLC intended to build the capacity to support science teaching and learning throughout a large regional education system. To frame the elements that we recommend as important considerations for leaders who are interested in forming a PLC similar to the Studygroup, we use Hord and Sommers's five components of PLCs. Each of the next five sections includes discussion of the strengths we brought and the challenges we faced with respect to each of these components.

Table 4.1. Shared Beliefs, Values, and Vision

Key aspects of this component for the Professional Development Studygroup:
• Foster a shared vision for effective teaching and learning (for students and their teachers), involving a learning theory–based instructional model.   • Understand and value that students and their teachers can develop conceptual understanding of science content and the nature of science by engaging in scientific inquiry.

Strengths	Challenges
The Studygroup's focus was on foundational knowledge and beliefs that are valuable in all education contexts (across grade levels K–16). Therefore, shared learning that focused on these knowledge and beliefs is relevant to all Studygroup members and promotes coherence in the vision for science teaching and learning across student, teacher, and professional development facilitator domains.	Beliefs about teaching and learning are fundamental and tightly held by educators. A shift to the learning theory–based instructional model required transformative changes in the Studygroup members' beliefs, values, and vision for effective teaching and learning, and this is harder for some than for others. *Inquiry* has widely varied meaning among educators, making a shared vision difficult to reach.

Shared Beliefs, Values, and Vision

Underpinning the Professional Development Studygroup was the conviction that the heart of the work is in the classroom, where students and teachers interact with science content in a complex interplay of teaching and learning. The vision for effective classroom teaching and learning then became the focus of professional learning for teachers, which in turn became the focus of Studygroup members. Figure 4.4 shows the graphical representation of our model, which was used to help Studygroup members build a shared vision and be metacognitive about the vision for each of these learning domains.

The value of this model is in how it explicitly conveys one of our foundational ideas: The goal of providing high-quality and coherent science teaching and

Figure 4.4. Teaching and Learning Domains Aligned With a Common Vision

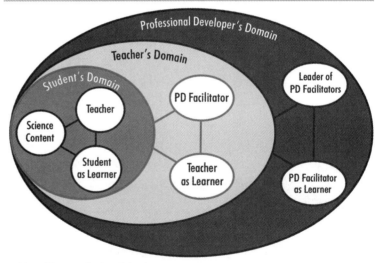

Note: PD = professional development.
Source: Adapted from Cohen and Ball 2000; Mumme and Seago 2002.

Chapter 4

learning is supported when all learners throughout the system experience well-aligned learning opportunities. Founded on this idea, Professional Development Studygroup sessions were never *trainings*; they were *learning opportunities* for professional development providers. All sessions were intentionally designed with the same learning theory–based instructional model as facilitators were expected to use in their own work designing and leading teacher professional learning. The specific instructional model that we used, the SCALE Immersion Model for Professional Learning, is discussed in the "Collective Learning and Its Application" section later in this chapter.

Developing shared beliefs, values, and vision among Studygroup members was accomplished by structuring the teaching and learning experiences that the PLC engaged in to mirror the vision for the teacher's and student's domains as shown in Figure 4.4. In other words, experiences for professional development facilitators (PLC members) focused on relevant content learning (e.g., understanding scientific inquiry) taught with pedagogical approaches that modeled the vision for both teacher professional development and science classroom experiences. The following quote from a Studygroup member who was a classroom teacher captures a glimpse of the vision for coherence we sought:

> It's as if something clicked [while I was co-facilitating], and I said to myself: Oh, I get it, not just facilitating, but I get teaching and what it's all about. I know that so many times, I have complained about how much I had to miss class for [the Professional Development Studygroup] and how it seemed to take away from my real job as a classroom teacher, but I see now that without this experience I wouldn't be even close to the teacher I am now.
>
> —*Megan Walzberg, sixth-grade math/science teacher,*
> *John Muir Middle School, LAUSD*

Table 4.2. Shared and Supportive Leadership

Key aspect of this component for the Professional Development Studygroup:
• Encourage *boundary crossers*, dedicated individuals with strong communication skills and the ability to empower others, from the partner universities and district through shared power and authority for making decisions and actively legitimizing the professional learning community (PLC) collaboration.

Strengths	Challenges
Partnership-based PLCs benefit from the rich contexts, resources, and expertise that members bring from different organizational cultures. In addition, a level of accountability to the overarching vision results from including PLC members from different contexts (there is less tendency to dwell on nonconstructive, organization-specific issues during meetings).	PLCs composed of two or more institutions, even different schools within the same district, need leaders who are able to operate effectively in the different cultures of the partnership to facilitate their coordination and ability to work toward shared goals.

Shared and Supportive Leadership

From their analysis of our science immersion work, including the Studygroup, Susan B. Millar and Matthew Clifford highlighted the critical role that a few individual leaders played as *boundary crossers*. From their 2005 memorandum titled "On 'Boundary Crossing' as a Key Attribute of Partnership Coordinators," we learn about key attributes these individuals tend to possess, which can be referenced as a guide for strategically selecting and encouraging the kind of leadership that is needed for a successful partnership-based PLC (S. B. Millar and M. Clifford, personal communication). Millar and Clifford's attribute analysis is included in Table 4.3.

Table 4.3. Attributes of Boundary Crossers

Organizational/structural attributes of a "boundary crosser" include
• access to, and the confidence of, high level decision-makers within one's home institution; • an extensive network of supportive, respectful colleagues within one's home organization; • capacity to focus the efforts of relevant staff and other resources on partnership activity; and • the authority or permission to devote enough time to one's partnership leader role to ensure that the boundary crosser does not act as a bottleneck that slows partnership work.

Personal attributes of a "boundary crosser" include

• deep commitment to the vision and goals of their own organization, and to the potential value of the expertise represented by other partner organizations; and
• organizational savvy, including
  ◦ ability to "mind the (partnership) shop"—to mind the partnership shop, a person must be able to keep the big vision for the partnership on colleagues' minds while also getting the nitty-gritty details done right and on time. It means having the creativity to secure the resources (crossing bureaucratic lines if necessary) needed to enable their organization to participate at the agreed upon level.
  ◦ ability to be "people and process smart" (Perkins 2003)—to be people and process smart entails having insight into, and respect for, each partner organization's strengths and limitations, and the capacity to use these insights during interaction with the other partner organization.
  ◦ ability to assess when existing organizational practices and structures are best, and when they are insufficient and must be improved;
  ◦ ability to learn through "creative abrasion" (Brown et al. 2005)—interactions that are abrasive enough to force learning for all participants require that the participants have important differences in expertise and experience, and that the participants interact in substantive ways about issues they jointly care about.
  ◦ ability to know when to take risks in ambiguous circumstances.

Elements of character exhibited by a "boundary crosser" include
• "can do" attitude and a thick skin. • willingness to take risks. • generosity in giving credit to others. • ability and willingness to work tirelessly.

Source: Millar, S. B., and M. Clifford. November 8, 2005. On "boundary crossing" as a key attribute of partnership coordinators. (personal communication)

The Studygroup benefited from a core team of boundary crossers who dedicated themselves to doing whatever it took to get the work done. The coordination required for the Studygroup's success could have been insurmountable without the collaboration among these effective boundary crossers. For other district science leaders or "change agents" interested in establishing PLCs for professional development facilitators—particularly if it involves partners from more than one institution—we

emphasize the importance of identifying individuals with boundary crosser attributes, delegating appropriate roles, and providing supportive conditions.

Table 4.4. Collective Learning and Its Application

Key aspects of this component for the Professional Development Studygroup:	
• Understand what the research and our collective experiences say about effective science teaching and learning for students, teachers, and preservice teachers. • Understand and be able to use the SCALE Immersion Model for Professional Learning (SIMPL) approach to professional development.	
Strengths	**Challenges**
The diverse experiences and backgrounds—brought to the group by elementary and secondary teacher leaders collaborating with science faculty, district science leadership, and education faculty—supported learning about both science concepts and pedagogy with input from diverse practitioners. The SIMPL approach to professional development strengthened alignment in what facilitators, teachers, and students experienced as learners, reinforcing the vision across contexts.	Because of the Professional Development Studygroup's strong commitment to its vision and goals, anyone who was uncomfortable with the inquiry approach to science teaching and learning and the Engage-Explore-Explain instructional design model (for *all* learners) had to confront these beliefs and forge co-facilitation agreements that aligned with this vision.

Collective Learning and Its Application

A hallmark of the Professional Development Studygroup is the SCALE Immersion Model for Professional Learning (SIMPL). It is an instructional design tool for those planning and providing learning opportunities for teachers and professional development facilitators. The SIMPL approach was a breakthrough that evolved from work the Studygroup lead facilitators did with the four SCALE district partners (and several other large districts in the nation). Until we developed and started using the SIMPL instructional model (linked to the nested ellipse diagram in Figure 4.4) to illustrate our intentions, we were unable to effectively model the vision for professional learning in the Studygroup such that it consistently transferred into the sessions our PLC members facilitated for teachers.

In Studygroup sessions, we needed to support coherence by both modeling the vision *and* making our instructional design and implementation explicit and visible so that learners could be metacognitive about the intentions (vision) and the theoretical underpinnings. The solution was the SIMPL approach, which mirrored for adult learners the Engage-Explore-Explain instructional model that was the vision for classroom instruction that aligned with research-based practices (Bransford, Brown, and Cocking 1999). In addition to mirroring the vision for students, SIMPL specifically apportioned time for the varied aspects of learning that effective professional development supports (e.g., learning new science content, pedagogy, and new instructional materials).

In the SIMPL approach for teacher-learners (Figure 4.5), participants begin with an *engage* experience, which elicits their prior conceptions about science content and/ or pedagogy that is relevant for teachers to understand and be able to use (to effectively

Figure 4.5. SCALE Immersion Model for Professional Learning (SIMPL) Approach for Teachers as Learners

Teacher's Lens: Explore

teach particular science concepts and/or employ strategies that align with the PLC vision). Next, the *exploring* occurs while teacher-learners participate as a student would in a lesson (e.g., a lesson from a Science Immersion Unit). By participating as a learner and suspending teacher thinking (not asking questions about teaching the lesson at this time), participants experience inquiry and other strategies and learn science concepts that they may never have experienced or learned before. Then, from this common context, the *explaining* is about the rationale for the lesson's science concepts and pedagogy, with time intentionally set aside for teacher-participants to reflect back on their initial conceptions (from the *engage* experience) and be metacognitive about their own learning. Through the SIMPL approach, teachers are intentionally given time and support for making conceptual changes in fundamental knowledge and beliefs about science teaching and learning. The SIMPL sequence is made visible, and facilitators explicitly indicate to participants what stage in the session is occurring at any given time.

Figure 4.6. SCALE Immersion Model for Professional Learning (SIMPL) Approach for Professional Development (PD) Facilitators as Learners

Teacher's Lens: Explore

PD Facilitator's *Teacher as Learner* Lens: Explore

The SIMPL approach for professional development facilitators (Figure 4.6) parallels the approach for teachers. To support the professional developer's learning, the *engage* experience is a time to focus and elicit prior conceptions about how to support teachers as learners with regard to a particular concept and/or pedagogy. Then, the *exploring* for the professional development facilitator is the entire session

that a teacher would experience with the SIMPL model (providing an opportunity to experience professional development designed with SIMPL and building a common experience for all participants). Finally, the *explaining* is about the rationale for the professional development session and, like SIMPL for teachers, includes explicit time for facilitators to reflect on their initial conceptions (from the *engage* experience) and be metacognitive about their experiences. The SIMPL approach used for facilitators sets clear expectations for learning theory–based professional learning by both modeling the way and using a tool to make the instructional design visible (see Figure 4.6).

During professional learning sessions (for teachers and for professional development providers), a poster of SIMPL was posted prominently so that an arrow could be physically moved to indicate which stage of the model was currently in play. In this way, SIMPL provided visibility for the instructional model underpinning our vision for science teaching and learning, while supporting effective learning experiences for adults. SIMPL was a valuable strategy for communicating and putting into practice aligned instructional approaches for the student's, teacher's, and professional developer's learning domains (see Figure 4.4).

Both professional developers and teacher-participants frequently voiced the value of the SIMPL approach. SCALE researchers studying science immersion effects on student learning also saw strong indications that SIMPL was an effective strategy for both motivating teachers to implement new materials and teaching teachers science content (Osthoff et al. 2007). Using SIMPL, we learned how to visibly articulate our expectations and increase the likelihood that the professional development our PLC members facilitated would be consistent across all grade levels in the district.

The following quotations offer insights into how two Professional Development Studygroup members felt about experiencing and applying the SIMPL model:

> I have participated in numerous professional development seminars and this is the first series in which I was given an opportunity to reflect and participate from various angles.
>
> *—Paul Narguizian, associate professor of biology education, CSU Los Angeles*

> The impact of the Professional Development Studygroup … is evident in the application of the SIMPL model to other professional development.
>
> *—Marlene Felix, director of elementary science and history, LAUSD*

Table 4.5. Supportive Conditions

Key aspects of this component for the Professional Development Studygroup:
• SCALE (System-wide Change for All Learners and Educators) and QED (Quality Educator Development) provided the meeting space, stipends, and logistical management and legitimized the structural factors (see Note 1) required by the Professional Development Studygroup.
• SCALE and QED provided the Studygroup's facilitators, who supported the learning community's norms and other relational factors (see Note 2).

Strengths	**Challenges**
The involvement of outside facilitators, made possible through SCALE and QED, offered broadened perspectives and unique opportunities. Funding for faculty release time and district stipends for Saturday workdays were also funded by QED and SCALE.	Coordinating the roles, responsibilities, and accountability for the structural and relational factors was challenging as the partnership formed and evolved.

Note 1: Structural factors are defined by Hord and Sommers (2008, p. 9) as the elements that "provide the physical requirements: time, place to meet for community work, resources and policies, etc. to support collaboration."

Note 2: Hord and Sommers (2008, p. 9) explain that relational factors "support the community's human and interpersonal development, openness, truth telling, and focusing on attitudes of respect and caring among the member."

Supportive Conditions

The district's and the university's commitments to the Professional Development Studygroup included monthly release time for PLC members and both direct and indirect recognition of the group's value. Having equivalent support contributed by three partners affected the Studygroup in an interesting way. It seems that once the partnership changed from a duo (LAUSD and UW) to a trio (adding CSU faculty), accountability heightened. Any commitment made was then noted by two, rather than one, other partners, which seemed to create greater resolve.

UW contributions through SCALE made it possible for the Professional Development Studygroup to delegate two individuals as lead facilitators and to strategically select outside consultants who helped establish a strong atmosphere of professionalism. The following quotation captures a sense of the community's professional norms, including the individual members' commitment:

> Participating in the SCALE/QED/LAUSD PD has taught me a lot. I have learned how vital it is to recognize the contributions of all participants; how important it is to know when to lead and when to provide support through facilitating discussions. I have in addition learned to place a lot of value on team building by providing constant nurturing and support to keep relationships going.

> Through my participation in this process, I learned that when people know that their views and contributions are valued, honored, and sought after, they would respond with a lot of commitment, hard work, and loyalty. And when people see their roles are critical, they will commit their whole

self to the effort. This is evident in the passion, sincerity and commitment exhibited by the study group members in the PD process.

— Irene Osisioma, science education faculty member, CSU Dominguez Hills

Table 4.6. Shared Personal Practice

Key aspect of this component for the Professional Development Studygroup:	
• Co-facilitation of the Professional Development Studygroup and its derivative professional development work was a unique and prominent professional learning community feature, requiring ongoing collegial reflection that supported both individual and collective improvement.	
Strengths	**Challenges**
Co-facilitation served as both a mentoring strategy for facilitators and an effective way to integrate educators' and scientists' perspectives for the Professional Development Studygroup and the teachers they facilitated.	Co-facilitation exposed an individual's knowledge and beliefs by putting them into practice. Further, this developed a shared understanding of how to co-facilitate; given that most educators work solo, this required new kinds of negotiations.

Shared Personal Practice

As a strategy for assuring that the professional development for teachers had both strong science-concept and pedagogical learning components, we committed early to having multiple facilitators, including scientists and educators. These diverse co-facilitation teams collaboratively planned and implemented science immersion sessions for teachers. In addition to providing important science content and pedagogical support for teacher participants, this co-facilitation strategy was used as a "lesson study" experience for the facilitators, who were putting into practice their learning from the Studygroup. Co-facilitation of professional development was like a lesson study because facilitators collaboratively prepared lessons for teachers (SIMPL sessions), implemented the sessions, and reflected together on what worked and what did not in light of evidence gathered about participants' understandings. In this way, co-facilitators were co-constructing their understanding of effective practices for supporting teachers as learners.

Science Immersion Institutes then became a critical motivator and context around which the Studygroup community clarified and enacted their beliefs, values, and vision. The institutes became a means for learning, rather than the culminating product. Thus, the additional costs associated with having four or five co-facilitators were justifiable because it was a valuable learning experience for both the teacher-participants and the professional developers.

Supporting integrated co-facilitation required intentional attention to complex issues that tend to be unfamiliar to educators who typically work in isolation. In the Professional Development Studygroup model for co-facilitation, everyone participated in all aspects of facilitating the institutes, regardless of their professional roles. To support this integration, Studygroup sessions prior to the summer institutes included explicit strategies to support growth stages, including forming, norming, storming, and effective performing (Tuckman 1965) among co-facilitation team members. For example, teams reviewed Garmston's "Presentation: Harmonious Duos" (2000) and drafted co-facilitation agreements before the summer institutes began.

The single most powerful strategy used by the Professional Development Studygroup to support effective co-facilitation turned out also to be the most valuable tool for confronting conflicting knowledge and beliefs about teaching and learning: *practice facilitation*. During a spring Studygroup meeting, co-facilitation teams were charged with preparing one 50-minute SIMPL session intended for use during their Science Immersion Institute. Then a round-robin schedule, using three or more rooms (with an assigned moderator) afforded each co-facilitation team time to implement their session, with peers serving as participants and critical friends.

Immediately following the practice session, the moderator guided a 15-minute reflection protocol to support metacognition about facilitation by both the co-facilitation team and their peer-participants. We learned from using this strategy that the academic discourse among Studygroup members about teaching and learning was often inconsistent with their actions. If we were to achieve coherence across learning domains and provide professional development with a clear message about our vision for science teaching and learning, it was pivotal to confront these strongly held beliefs about what constitutes the most effective way to plan and execute teaching strategies.

Practice facilitation became the catalyst for PLC members to share their knowledge and beliefs openly as they designed and co-facilitated sessions for their peers. Through these practical application experiences and facilitated reflections, Studygroup members began challenging conversations about their approaches to teaching and learning. In addition, practice facilitation provided participant-peers with opportunities to experience learning facilitated by their colleagues and listen to their colleagues' reflections about their practices. In this way, practice facilitation gave PLC members multiple and varied experiences of professional learning on which to collaboratively build their beliefs about effective practices. Not surprisingly, practice facilitation turned out to be the most commonly cited strategy when Studygroup members discussed what had the greatest effect on their personal practices.

The quotation below illustrates the trust and professional focus that Studygroup members grew to share as a result of their experiences in their learning community.

One of the strengths of the process was the connection we made at the personal level so that we felt comfortable being critical of each other ... We had common goals and we allowed for our differences so they became assets to the process. The spring [professional development] provided the time necessary to build this foundation. During the week of the institutes

our comfort level allowed us to incorporate a flexibility that is hard to do with people you are not comfortable with, so that when [necessary] we could quickly alter our direction and keep the experience a positive one for the participants.

—*Virginia Vandergon, associate professor in biology, CSU Northridge*

Conclusion

The Professional Development Studygroup, which developed through a partnership among universities and LAUSD, demonstrated how a K–16 learning community could be composed of a cross-institutional cadre of professional development facilitators. With this broadened view of a PLC, its vision expanded to include a goal of aligning the vision and experiences for students, preservice and inservice teachers, and professional development facilitators. Simultaneously, the Studygroup built a capable cadre of professional development providers for LAUSD. This Studygroup developed a shared vision of inquiry and the SIMPL approach to professional development, resulting in ongoing improvements in the overall professional development system to prepare teachers to teach inquiry-based science units. Because of the middle-out approach taken to establish the Studygroup, the PLC's work was grounded in classroom practice and the group's intellectual gains will remain with the region's practitioners, regardless of the administration turnover that is typical in urban districts.

During the final year of the SCALE project, the superintendent of LAUSD changed, and there were significant shifts in UW support and CSU leadership. The philosophy of centralizing the educational experience for teachers and students across the eight local districts in LAUSD shifted to each local district assuming control of the professional development and curricula to meet the needs of their district constituents. Even with this change in overall district policy, the members of the Studygroup continue to move their common vision forward through local districts with support from the academic instructors and district superintendents. This is evident as new curriculum materials come into the districts and are implemented within the framework we co-constructed. Further, Studygroup members at the local universities are structuring undergraduate classes and inservice outreach programs to reflect the PLC's vision for inquiry, and they are using the SIMPL approach to professional development. Our middle-out approach to science teaching and learning improvement appears to have created enough institutional knowledge that it is sustainable for the foreseeable future through the individual and institutional PLC partners.

From the Professional Development Studygroup's experiences as a learning community, we offer a viable example for educators who want to support holistic improvements in teacher professional learning. What the Studygroup taught us is that PLCs can effectively support professional development providers and university faculty to improve teacher learning. We encourage others to consider the value of using this type of PLC to collaboratively build expertise and develop the system-wide coherence needed to address the concerns represented in the opening vignette about Ms. Wake's teaching experiences.

Reflection Questions
- How would you describe your own culture regarding collaboration across educational institutions in your region?
- How do K–12 educators and university science and science education faculty communicate and respond to each other?
- What kind of cross-institutional culture was developed in the chapter? How close to, or far away from, that kind of culture is your organization?
- What would it take to move closer toward a culture that supports and sustains PLCs that comprise a broad range of educators in your region?
- Who can you identify as potential boundary crossers, and what are their strengths and weaknesses?

References

Bransford, J. D., A. L. Brown, and R. R. Cocking, eds. 1999. *How people learn: Brain, mind, experience, and school.* Washington, DC: National Academies Press.

Brown, J. S., S. Denning, K. Groh, and L. Prusak. 2005. *Storytelling in organizations: Why storytelling is transforming 21st century organizations and management.* Burlington, MA: Elsevier Butterworth-Heinemann.

Clifford, M., and S. B. Millar. 2007. *K–20 partnership: A definition and proof of concept.* WCER Working Paper 2007–9. Madison, WI: Wisconsin Center for Education Research. *www.wcer.wisc.edu/publications/workingPapers/Working_Paper_No_2007_09.swf*

Cohen, D. K., and D. L. Ball. 2000. *Instructional innovation: Reconsidering the story,* p. 5. The Study of Instructional Improvement Working Paper. Ann Arbor: University of Michigan.

Garmston, R. 2000. Presentation: Harmonious duos. *Journal of Staff Development* 21 (2): 65–67.

Hord, S. M., and W. A. Sommers. 2008. *Leading professional learning communities: Voices from research and practice.* Thousand Oaks, CA: Corwin Press.

Mumme, J., and N. Seago. 2002. Issues and challenges in facilitating video cases for mathematics professional development. Paper presented at the annual meeting of the American Educational Research Association, New Orleans.

Osthoff, E., C. Clune, P. White, J. Ferrare, K. Kretchmar, and K. Kelly. 2007. *Tentative findings of the SCALE study of middle school immersion in LAUSD: A conversation with LAUSD professional development facilitators.* Madison, WI: University of Wisconsin—Madison, Wisconsin Center for Education Research. *www.scalemsp.org/files/research/Products/SCALE_Gr_Immersion_Study_Yr_5_report.pdf*

Perkins, D. 2003. *King Arthur's round table: How collaborative conversations create smart organizations.* San Francisco: John Wiley and Sons.

Tuckman, Bruce. 1965. Developmental sequence in small groups. *Psychological Bulletin* 63: 384–399.

Chapter 5

Creating and Sustaining Science-Focused Professional Learning Communities Through Partnerships

Carolyn Landel and George Nelson

"Establishing a professional learning community within a school does not occur quickly or spontaneously. It requires dedicated and intentional effort on the part of the administrator and the professional staff."

—Melanie Morrissey, *Professional Learning Communities: An Ongoing Exploration* (2000, p. 4)

Chapter 5

Teacher collaboration through professional learning communities (PLCs) is emerging as a key element in instructional improvement. Our definition of a PLC is a group of educators prepared and supported to work regularly and collaboratively to develop the necessary knowledge and skills to improve instructional effectiveness and student outcomes (DuFour and Eaker 1998). Effective PLCs are rooted in the subjects teachers teach, are relevant and applicable to the practice of teaching, and are focused on student learning issues defined by the group members as evidenced by student work. In this context PLCs provide opportunities for teachers to think and work collectively to identify and address instructional problems and adjust their practice in response to their specific classroom contexts (NRC 2007; Loucks-Horsley et al. 2003).

For PLCs to have a positive impact on science instruction, their work must necessarily provide participating teachers a means to develop a deep knowledge of the science content they teach, of the ways in which children come to develop their understanding of selected scientific concepts, and of content-specific instructional and assessment strategies to support learning for each student. Teacher leaders have long been viewed as critical contributors to creating and leading PLCs so that all teachers can advance along a lifelong professional learning continuum (Elmore 2000).

The North Cascades and Olympic Science Partnership (NCOSP) supported over 150 teachers in Washington through a five-year experience to become teacher leaders effective in their own instructional practices, and also effective at engaging their peers in PLCs to enhance instruction throughout their buildings and transform their science education program. The work of NCOSP provides a view of PLCs in two contexts—within the larger multi-institutional partnership itself and within the individual schools the partnership supported. In this chapter we share selected components of the NCOSP model for PLCs and the impact those communities had on instruction and student learning. We offer examples from partner districts to illustrate how the program was enacted in a representative elementary and secondary setting. We close with some valuable lessons learned that might help others blazing new paths in developing PLCs that support effective science instruction.

Begin With a Partnership

NCOSP represents a partnership in which all members engage in sharing responsibility, expertise, and effort to improve student learning in science. NCOSP includes among its partners five higher education institutions and 28 school districts in northwest Washington. The partnership engages disciplinary science faculty from five higher education institutions and K–12 teachers and administrators from the school districts to access the relevant expertise each offers to address the challenges of science education reform. Creating a K–12-higher education partnership may seem far removed from forming PLCs in K–12 schools, but this work strengthens and deepens the commitment to a shared vision for improving student success in science. Developing a partnership also paves the way for learning to work collaboratively and valuing and accessing needed resources and expertise from diverse sources.

In the case of NCOSP, activities planned in the earliest days of the proposal-writing process and implemented in the first year of the project helped all partners collectively shape and embrace the partnership goals. At the same time, the partners collaboratively constructed a set of principles to articulate the values and beliefs within which the project would work to achieve those goals (see Figure 5.1). PLC structure and ways of operating were also introduced to help shape norms for communication and group work (Garmston and Wellman 1999). These efforts brought all partners together around a shared vision for the outcomes of the partnership, and as a way of working to achieve that end. Their shared goal was to improve outcomes for every student in science through the long-term efforts of PLCs. Their shared beliefs demanded that their goal be achieved in a way that all partners participated as learners, contributed to and benefited from participation, respected the diverse contributions and needs of all members, applied or conducted meaningful research, and used time and resources effectively.

Figure 5.1. Summary of North Cascades and Olympic Science Partnership (NCOSP) Guiding Principles

1. *Organizing Principle:* The project is organized and managed to achieve its goals on time and within the budget.
2. *Research Principle:* Actions will be planned and modified based on the best research. Where no prior research is available, careful research will be designed and carried out.
3. *Learning Principle:* Everyone in the project is a learner.
4. *Equity Principle:* There are clear, high, and realistic expectations for all learners, regardless of differences, in an inclusive, supportive environment.
5. *Collaboration Principle:* NCOSP is a true partnership. Each partner contributes to and benefits from achieving the goals.

Note: A detailed description of the guiding principles is on the NCOSP website: www.ncosp.wwu.edu/projectgoals/principles.cfm.

This sense of partnership provided a strong foundation for working together as an effective multi-institutional learning community. Evidence from surveys, interviews, and observations revealed that the higher education faculty profited greatly from interactions with K–12 teachers, as well as among themselves. They better understood the day-to-day struggles of the work of K–12 teachers and learned more strategies for teaching diverse students in their own science courses. K–12 teachers came to recognize that higher education faculty face many of the same challenges and dilemmas in their efforts to improve instruction. Together, K–12 teachers and higher education faculty came to value the knowledge and experience each offered and appreciate the opportunity to work together to solve complex problems in teaching and learning.

Chapter 5

Focus on Science Content and Content-Specific Pedagogy

Inherent to the work of NCOSP is the belief that to make science accessible to all learners, K–12 teachers and higher education faculty alike need a strong understanding of the subject matter, an appreciation for how students learn, and a repertoire of appropriate instructional strategies to engage students' prior ideas and build more accurate understanding of science (Bransford, Brown, and Cocking 1999; Schulman 1986). The core of the NCOSP program is a series of 80-hour residential summer academies for emerging teacher leaders to enhance their knowledge of effective instruction, assessment, and collaboration. Each academy includes a carefully designed content immersion to improve content knowledge and reinforce conceptual, constructivist science teaching strategies (see Table 5.1). Additional experiences provide support for implementing these new instructional strategies in the classroom and developing knowledge among peers.

Table 5.1. North Cascades and Olympic Science Partnership Summer Professional Development Major Themes

	Year 1	Year 2	Year 3	Years 4–5
Science Content	Flow of Matter and Energy in Physical Systems	Flow of Matter and Energy in Living Systems	Flow of Matter and Energy in Earth Systems	Teacher Leader and Administrator Planning
Major Themes	*Science of Learning*: Implications for teaching and learning *Planning for Continuous Improvement*: Action plans focused on individual classroom practice *Professional Learning Community*: Elements of professional learning community	*Science of Learning*: Implications for different student populations *Planning for Continuous Improvement*: Collaborative practices focused on student learning *Professional Learning Community*: Collaborative networks across districts	*Science of Learning*: From theory to practice *Planning for Continuous Improvement*: District coherence through a focus on shared goals for student learning *Professional Learning Community*: Leadership and facilitation of collaborative groups	Beyond the teacher leader… Supporting and sustaining a school-based professional learning community

Note: Detailed Summer Academy agendas and resources can be found at *www.ncosp.wwu.edu*.

In the first year of the NCOSP program, teacher leaders engaged as learners in tested, inquiry-based physical science curricula.[1] Life science and Earth science content immersion experiences developed by the NCOSP faculty[2] followed in the second and third years to provide authentic inquiry experiences in a diverse array of scientific topics commonly taught in the K–12 curriculum. The immersions guided participating teacher leaders through a structured sequence of writing prompts, experiments, data analyses, and discussions to build a more scientifically accurate understanding

---

[1] The inquiry-based physical science curricula included F. Goldberg, S. Robinson, and V. Otero, *Physics and Everyday Thinking* (Armonk, NY: It's About Time, 2008); and L. C. McDermott, *Physics by Inquiry* (New York: John Wiley and Sons, 1996).

[2] Recent versions of the Earth and life science curricula developed by the faculty can be viewed on the NCOSP website: *www.ncosp.wwu.edu/Resources/Summer2007PD/Instruction/II%20Prior%20Ideas/C.%20Eliciting%20Student%20Ideas/Life%20Science%20Curriculum.pdf*.

of relevant big ideas within each scientific discipline. Through a carefully constructed learning cycle, consistent with constructivist learning theory, ideas were developed over time with increasing sophistication. Facilitators continuously conducted formative assessments embedded through both written and oral exercises to monitor content understanding and inform instruction. New ideas were introduced as teachers demonstrated the prerequisite knowledge needed to proceed.

In addition to providing subject-specific content experiences, the immersion sessions introduced the book *How People Learn* (Bransford, Brown, and Cocking 1999) as a unifying framework for learning and modeled this framework in the context of the content experiences. Explicit discussions of pedagogical strategies consistent with that framework were embedded within the content sessions, sometimes supplemented with video recordings of naive student conceptions of the content under consideration. Supporting sessions provided teachers time to identify opportunities to improve implementation of their own science instructional materials through careful application of research-based pedagogy supported by *How People Learn*.

These experiences combined to develop a strong and shared vision of effective instruction among participating NCOSP higher education and K–12 faculty and resulted in improved instructional effectiveness in science classrooms at all levels. Assessments of content knowledge administered to teacher leaders at each Summer Academy showed significant increases from pretest to posttest, as well as retention as measured by delayed posttests one year later. Year after year, through interviews and surveys, both K–12 teachers and higher education faculty consistently reported that the content immersions and focus on *How People Learn* had the greatest influence on their knowledge and instructional practice. Classroom observations were conducted in both K–12 and undergraduate classrooms using the protocol developed by Horizon Research (Weiss et al. 2003). The results were consistent with self-report data and showed continuous improvements in strategies modeled and explored during the immersion sessions.

After completing three years of NCOSP professional development experiences, modest but significant improvements in student performance on the state science assessment, compared with their demographically matched counterparts, were detectable for students who had a teacher leader for one year of instruction. Additional improvements occurred when students had two or more years of instruction from one or more teacher leaders, demonstrating a positive, value-added effect (see Figures 5.2 and 5.3). Hispanic students, students of poverty, special education students, and students with limited mathematics proficiency showed even larger gains in teacher leader classrooms (see Figure 5.4).

Figure 5.2. Students with more contact with North Cascades and Olympics Science Partnership (NCOSP) teacher leaders (TLs) show higher levels of proficiency on the 2007 Science Washington Assessment of Student Learning in fifth and tenth grades.

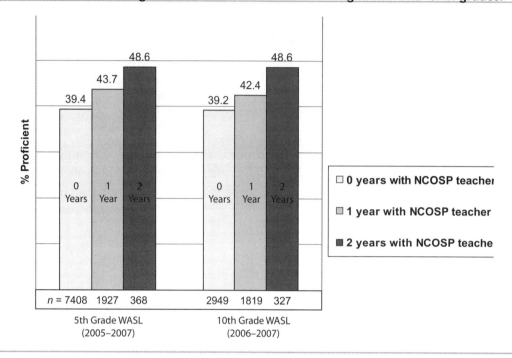

Figure 5.3. Students with more contact with North Cascades and Olympic Science Partnership (NCOSP) teacher leaders show greater mean gains from the eighth grade (2005) to the tenth grade (2007) on the Science Washington Assessment of Student Learning.

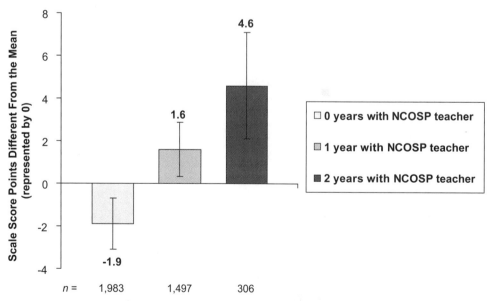

Note: The mean gain score for the 3,786 students was -8.7 scale score points.

National Science Teachers Association

Figure 5.4. Several subgroup populations score higher on the 2005–2007 Science Washington Assessment of Student Learning with North Cascades and Olympic Science Partnership teacher leaders.

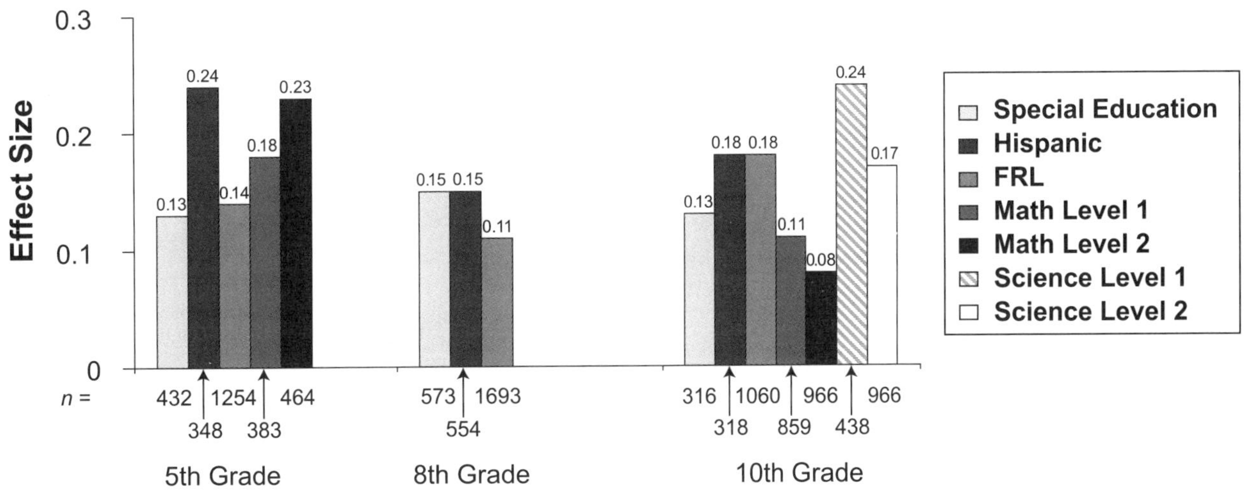

Notes: Effect sizes of the differences were calculated using the means and standard deviations. FRL = free or reduced-price lunch.

Support Teacher and Administrator Leadership

In addition to deepening teacher content and pedagogical content knowledge, NCOSP programs and activities build the knowledge and skills that teacher leaders, administrators, and higher education faculty need to support collaborative groups focused on student learning. In the first year, the partnership focused participating teachers on their individual goals for instructional improvements based on modeling provided by facilitators. In this way, teacher leaders were given time to reflect on and refine their personal practice before being asked to lead or facilitate change for others.

In the second year, experiences were aimed at helping teacher leaders develop skills in supporting collaborative groups focused on student learning. The second year provided time for teacher leaders to explore PLC norms and protocols introduced earlier and to increase their confidence and proficiency in applying them (Garmston and Wellman 1999). Expectations for establishing collaborations were initially confined to working with other participating teacher leaders, administrators, and faculty who shared the partnership beliefs and knowledge base.

In the third year, working collaboratively remained a focus, but with an emphasis on examining student work for evidence of instruction resulting in the desired learning outcomes for students. A number of protocols for examining student work were explored, as well as strategies for knowing how to select an appropriate

protocol given the desired outcome. Teacher leaders were also provided experiences to develop their proficiency at facilitating collaborative groups, not just participating in them, in preparation for their transition to becoming PLC leaders in their buildings. The sum of these experiences prepared teacher leaders to

- make links to specific content, developmental appropriateness, and curriculum coherence (AAAS 2001a, 2001b);
- apply research on student conceptions (Driver et al. 1994) and instructional strategies to state and national standards;
- use classroom assessments to improve instruction (Black and Wiliam 1998, Black et al. 2004);
- use classroom observation instruments to assess instructional practices (Piburn and Sawada 2000; Weiss 1999); and
- use protocols to examine and score student work and apply them in school-based learning communities (Loucks-Horsley et al. 2003).

At the same time, expectations for participation by administrators increased to ensure they were ready and prepared to incorporate models of teacher leadership into their school-based professional development activities to engage other teachers in their buildings. During the third year of the program, Teacher Leader-Administrator Symposia were offered throughout the school year to provide teacher leaders and principals opportunities for learning and reflection on the challenges they faced in supporting and sustaining effective PLCs. These symposia helped teacher leaders and principals continue to develop a shared understanding of effective instruction, assessment, and collaboration. Time was allotted during each symposium for participants to clarify their respective roles in supporting PLCs and to generate short- and long-term action plans for implementing PLCs into their normal school schedule.

Data collected at the close of the third year of the program show a striking coalescence among all partners regarding the value and impact of NCOSP. Teachers and administrators alike reported improvements in multiple aspects of their science education programs over the previous three years and attributed virtually all of the changes to their involvement in NCOSP. Significant areas of change attributed mostly to NCOSP included knowledge and skills of teaching science, a common coherent vision of quality science instruction, and staff collaboration around science. Teachers and administrators also expressed appreciation for and confidence in the continued existence of a reliable community of science educators with shared values regarding science reform and common practices around collaboration. This context created the will among partner schools to continue with their efforts to institute PLCs and provide more teachers with the opportunity to participate, contribute, and benefit in partnership activities. Investing three years into laying this groundwork established a state of readiness among all stakeholders—administrators, teacher leaders, and other teachers—to implement a new way of working together through PLCs and to be successful in doing so.

Balance Support With Accountability

For three years the partnership focused on intensive professional development experiences in science content, instructional strategies, and leadership practices. Higher education faculty, teacher leaders, and administrators were prepared to establish or strengthen PLCs within the partner schools, including working with teachers with little or no prior experience with NCOSP programs and activities. The fourth year of the NCOSP program design reflected a readiness among these leaders to move into effective implementation and capitalized on the knowledge and skills they had collectively developed. This allowed participating schools to extend the professional development benefits and partnership with higher education afforded by NCOSP to more teachers, to ground professional development within the school and the existing science curricula, to integrate the science professional development with other curricular areas, and to pave the way for institutionalizing sustainable PLCs focused on student learning.

Continued participation into the fourth year of NCOSP activities required collaboration between teacher leaders and principals and a commitment to include additional teachers in PLC activities over the next academic year. Through an application process, partner schools were asked to demonstrate how their teachers, together with their teacher leader and their principal, would form a PLC. Each school-based team was asked to define the content learning needs of both the teachers and students and how they would use the district science curricula to focus on science content and instructional strategies to help teachers and students learn the selected topics. A group of faculty, staff, and K–12 teachers on special assignment (TOSAs) reviewed all the applications for completeness, clarity, and quality using a collaboratively constructed rubric. Each school was given feedback based on that review and provided access to TOSAs, faculty, and staff for clarification and technical assistance to ensure they were successful, while still meeting high expectations for quality.

The partnership stood ready to support schools in their efforts to take this next step in implementation and expand their reach to other teachers. NCOSP provided time and resources for a summer planning week for teacher leaders, administrators, and partner higher education disciplinary science faculty. The planning week opened with a "fishbowl" activity where a group of teacher leaders and a partner faculty conducted a PLC meeting that involved examining student work while all other participants were gathered around as observers. The quality of the simulated meeting strengthened the group's shared vision of PLCs and provided

Chapter 5

an example to compare and contrast with their prior PLC work. During the planning week, participants collaboratively designed three-day content- and pedagogy-focused professional development experiences to initiate their emerging PLCs. The designs were influenced by the opening fishbowl simulation and subsequently created using an electronic Professional Development Planning Tool provided by NCOSP. This tool was an index to the many articles, PowerPoints, handouts, and facilitation outlines from the programs provided for teacher leaders during their previous three years of preparation, and it resulted in them feeling more prepared to use these resources to assist their colleagues. This tool was powerful in terms of the assurance and confidence it gave the teacher leaders by reminding them of their own learning experiences and providing the resources for them to use with others.

The three-day programs were provided for teachers within their local schools later that summer, before the start of the school year. Though teacher leaders all drew on a common set of NCOSP resources for their designs, no two agendas were identical. As we had hoped, the teacher leaders purposefully modified the resources appropriately to reflect their relationships with their colleagues and their understanding of their local context. Document analysis of the agendas revealed that over 90% of the three-day programs included providing some form of abbreviated "content immersion," usually in collaboration with the partner higher education faculty. Nearly 80% included experiences for participants to explore the key findings from *How People Learn* and elements of effective PLCs.

From 137 groups that had previously participated in NCOSP professional development programs, 111 submitted successful applications to establish PLCs within their schools to reach a new cohort of teachers with little or no prior experience with NCOSP. In surveys collected at the conclusion of the planning week, over 90% of teacher leaders indicated that they felt "prepared" or "very prepared" to lead their PLC by their cumulative experiences as teacher leaders in the first three years of the project. Document analysis of the three-day designs showed that NCOSP TOSAs and partner faculty used the materials effectively and documented their use of NCOSP tools. The implementation of the three-day program was judged to be effective as evidenced by satisfaction surveys from PLC members and observations of a sampling of PLC workshops. Activity logs and surveys collected during the following year revealed that most teacher leaders continued to facilitate their PLC effectively with the support of their principal and NCOSP TOSAs and higher education faculty.

Increased Participation

As the fifth year approached, NCOSP focused on broadening its impact by inviting the teachers from the newly formed PLCs to participate in extended summer experiences. The positive impact of partnership activities on teacher knowledge, practice, and student outcomes, as well as improvements in administrative support and school capacity, created significant interest in and demand for intensive content- and pedagogy-focused experiences. The new PLC members who had just begun their work with their teacher leaders were invited to a weeklong program to deepen their knowledge of findings from research on *How People Learn*, science content relevant to teaching, how students learn science, and instructional strategies that support student learning. During the program, participants also applied their new knowledge to the instructional materials they teach. Selected sessions were scheduled jointly with NCOSP teacher leaders and administrators to inform the work of their PLCs during the next academic year.

Teacher leaders and administrators still sought structured planning time to prepare for their roles in supporting PLCs during the academic year. A three-day program to deepen their understanding of effective science instruction and PLCs and to generate a plan for continued support of their PLCs was offered to strengthen and sustain this leadership cadre. Sessions were held jointly with PLC members to allow for collaborative planning and decision making. District administrators participated on the final day, and this provided teacher leaders and principals the opportunity to share their plans and demonstrate how they met the needs of their unique school context and supported the professional development goals of the district.

Over 350 teachers who were new to the PLCs participated in NCOSP summer experiences, and 100 participants, including teacher leaders and principals, attended the Teacher Leader-Administrator Planning program. After the summer experiences, 80% of the participants reported that their PLCs will continue to work on improving science teaching and learning during the school year (99% responded that it was "somewhat likely" or "very likely" that their PLC would continue). The most common reasons reported for the PLCs continuing were teacher buy-in and commitment, teacher motivation to improve science teaching and learning, knowledgeable and committed leaders, and the collaborative atmosphere of the PLC. Teacher leaders and administrators reported that they valued the protocols and planning resources that helped them organize and focus their work and the research presentations that helped them understand school values, beliefs, and capacities that contribute to effective teaching and learning.

Examples From Practice

There is no single ideal manifestation of successful PLCs in school buildings. Though all participating school leaders experienced the same core NCOSP program, PLC implementation varied within each school setting. Here, through the voices of participating teacher leaders, we share how two very different schools applied the knowledge and skills developed through NCOSP to support school improvement. In one example, leadership came from the top down, while in the

other it was built from the bottom up. Both are resulting in improved school culture and student achievement through the focused work of PLCs. Though the stories told below do not detail daily, weekly, and monthly PLC activities, they do offer a glimpse of the transformations that resulted and suggest what is possible if educators are prepared and supported to implement PLCs.

Nooksack Elementary School

Nooksack Elementary is a small rural school on the Canadian border in northwest Washington. Of the 272 students in grades K–5, 44% are female, 56% are male, 24% are Hispanic, 17% are transitional bilingual, 15% are identified with special needs, and 55% receive free or reduced-price lunch.

A gifted principal, who came to embrace collaboration and a focus on individual student success later in her career, led the school. She retired last year after training her successor, a former NCOSP teacher leader.

In the NCOSP baseline year (2003–2004), 41.5% of the fifth-grade students were proficient or above on the state science assessment. In 2007–2008, the fifth-grade teachers reported:

> Forty-three out of forty-four fifth-grade students at Nooksack Elementary (97.8%) met or exceeded standards on the Science Washington Assessment of Student Learning. All fifth-grade students took the test and students who passed included all special education students, all ELL students, and all migrant/bilingual students. Nooksack Elementary fifth-grade teachers attribute this success rate to three main factors: system-wide adaptive changes in both beliefs and practices by all stakeholders, the use of student-involved assessment practices in all subjects, and deliberate, focused technical changes in science curriculum and instruction targeted to improve student learning.

The teachers also stated in this report that "at Nooksack Elementary, we have spent years learning new ways of working together and developing shared beliefs around teaching, learning, and achievement. **We believe that teacher collaboration and shared beliefs underlie the high achievement that we are seeing from all students in all subjects in all grades.**" [emphasis added][3]

Markishtum Middle School/Neah Bay High School

Phillip Renault is an experienced middle school science teacher at Markishtum Middle School. He is also an NCOSP teacher leader who is earning his master's degree in science education at Western Washington University, supported by

---

[3] B. Herzog, J. Heutink, and T. Lankhaar, "Nooksack Elementary School: Grade Five Science WASL Success Factors" (unpublished internal report, 2008).

NCOSP. Markishtum Middle School/Neah Bay High School is located on the Makah Indian Reservation on the very northwest tip of the Olympic Peninsula. It has 161 students in grades 6–12, of whom 94% are Native American, 64% are eligible for free or reduced-price meals, and 17% are identified with special needs. Here is Phil's story:

> District-wide, there had been concerns about teachers not having time to work together, to have teacher directed collaboration. Traditionally our extra non-student days have been filled with workshops on subjects like Discipline, Poverty, School Climate, Gangs, but little time was given for teacher-to-teacher collaboration. Teachers decided it was time to ask for specific time to be set aside to collaborate among ourselves, time that was guaranteed by our contract. Contract negotiations took place and we were given a half day a month specifically for teacher directed collaboration.

> I imagine that from an administrator's point of view questions then start to emerge. What is teacher collaboration? What does it look like? Is there evidence that one approach works better than another?

> As if to answer these questions, NCOSP provided our middle school teachers with the opportunity to work together to develop a vision and to create in a formal sense a PLC. We had a chance to demonstrate what teacher collaboration could look like using the ideas from NCOSP and create a Professional Learning Community. In fact the time needed to do this throughout the school year was negotiated into our contract. As a middle school teacher, it is exciting to be able to maintain a sense of independence, a recognition that the middle school student body is different from the other ages, and as such, needs to have independence from the type of structure other grades have.

> To start things off more slowly, we decided to present a three-day summer workshop examining the *How People Learn* research. We had a mini-lesson on what this might look like in the science classroom. We talked about utilizing notebooks across the curriculum and how that might look. We then looked at PLCs and came up with activities we could do as a PLC. We decided to use our teacher directed collaborative release days to look at student work. The idea is that to begin to integrate classes, we need to know more about what others are doing as well as what our students' abilities in the various subjects are. To this end we are looking at student work using protocols developed through NCOSP. We pursued this throughout the school year and are working on how to proceed next.[4]

---

[4] P. Renault, "What are we doing today? (or what is being done to us today?)" (unpublished NCOSP case study, 2008).

Chapter 5

From 2004 to 2008, passing rates at Markishtum/Neah Bay on the 8th-grade science Washington Assessment of Student Learning have risen from 19% to 47%, the state average, and at the 10th-grade level, they have gone from 0% to 48%, 8% above the state average.

Lessons Learned

Evaluation findings collected over five years through NCOSP, and the insights gained from the two sample schools, point to several factors important to establishing successful PLCs. First, focusing on content and instruction in the context of a broad-based partnership cannot be overlooked in a rushed attempt to establish PLCs. A partnership brings together the array of stakeholders needed to be successful in the daunting task of improving learning outcomes for each student. By working together, both teacher leaders and higher education faculty learn science content out of their different areas of prior study. Administrators and teacher leaders learn to trust each other and work together to improve instructional leadership in schools and to support other teachers as they learn. All partners learn research-based pedagogical practices from preparing and teaching together and from co-developing tools they can later use to support PLC experiences.

These initial experiences as learners of science, the discussions around pedagogical strategies that support learning, and the collaborative environment created to support them all serve to foreshadow the conversations that are at the heart of effective PLCs. Without this core, PLCs can too easily become all "style" but no "substance"—a structured routine or mechanical set of procedures members follow, but no reflective dialogue that will generate instructional improvements or support struggling students.

Implementing effective PLCs also requires patience tempered with perseverance. The urge to act quickly often supersedes the need to implement carefully. PLCs require more than a time and place to meet if they are to achieve their promise of improving student outcomes. Schools often abandon a new strategy after a year—or maybe two—because "it didn't work." The lack of positive results is all too often a result of poor implementation, not of inherent flaws in the strategy itself. A three-year trajectory provides teacher leaders and administrators with the necessary experiences and collection of effective tools in leadership and facilitation to enable them to successfully develop and support PLCs. Nooksack Elementary recognized the timeline required and reaped the benefits of their diligence in long-term continuous student achievement gains. There simply are no shortcuts, and attempts to find them serve only to detract from the focused, long-term effort needed to support student success.

Increasingly, teachers are being held accountable to improve their practice and student performance. Expectations for these kinds of positive results are only reasonable—and achievable—when they come with the support needed to improve. Teachers need and deserve access to resources—human, time, material, and financial—to make the fundamental changes in their individual and collective practice necessary to have a lasting impact on each student's educational experience. By the same token, time and resources have all too often been allocated to activities without expectations for improvement or evidence of change. Schools cannot afford to continue to allocate their limited resources to sustain the status quo that is failing so many students. Reciprocity (Elmore 2005) requires resources to be allocated—but with strings attached. Change for the better must result. Both the Nooksack Elementary and Markishtum Middle School cases show us that focused and continuous dialogue among skilled and thoughtful teachers and administrators to negotiate the required support and to define reasonable expectations is necessary to ensure that PLCs remain on course to improve student learning.

Teacher leader initiatives are often criticized because they invest heavily in a small number of individuals and the benefits never extend beyond this "inner circle." Success for each student requires careful preparation of teacher leaders and administrators coupled with a long-term plan for supporting their work with others. The Neah Bay example illustrates what is possible when student-focused teacher collaboration becomes a routine part of the contractual workday for knowledgeable and dedicated teachers. In the end, when their work is purposefully implemented in the context of a partnership that values and accesses the diverse experience and expertise of all its members, sustainable PLCs can be created and improved student learning follows.

Reflection Questions
- Does your own content knowledge or that of a colleague ever limit the ability of your PLC to provide effective instruction or diagnose student thinking? How often do your PLC meetings explicitly address developing science content knowledge? How could your PLC safely and effectively better support teachers to learn science content relevant to teaching?
- What expertise exists within your PLC? What expertise is lacking? What "partners" are accessible to your PLC to provide additional knowledge? What steps can you take to reach out to potential partners?
- What resources—human, financial, material—are allocated for your PLC work? What results are expected for that investment of resources? Is the investment well matched with the expectations? What conversations can you have, and with whom, to negotiate for an equitable distribution of resources in exchange for clear, measurable, and positive outcomes?

Chapter 5

References

American Association for the Advancement of Science (AAAS). 2001a. *Atlas of science literacy.* Washington, DC: AAAS.

American Association for the Advancement of Science (AAAS). 2001b. *Designs for science literacy.* Washington, DC: AAAS.

Black, P., and D. Wiliam. 1998. Inside the black box: Raising standards through classroom assessment. *Phi Delta Kappan* 80 (2): 139–148.

Black, P., C. Harrison, C. Lee, B. Marshall, and D. Wiliam. 2004. Working inside the black box: Assessment for learning in the classroom. *Phi Delta Kappan* 86 (1): 9–21.

Bransford, J. D., A. L. Brown, and R. R. Cocking, eds. 1999. *How people learn: Brain, mind, experience, and school.* Washington, DC: National Academy Press.

Driver, R., A. Squires, P. Rushworth, and V. Wood-Robinson. 1994. *Making sense of secondary science.* New York: Routledge, Taylor and Francis.

DuFour, R., and R. Eaker. 1998. *Professional learning communities at work: Best practices for enhancing student achievement.* Bloomington, IN: National Educational Service.

Elmore, R. F. 2000. *Building a new structure for school leadership.* Washington, DC: Albert Shanker Institute.

Elmore, R. F. 2005. *School reform from the inside out: Policy, practice, and performance.* Cambridge, MA: Harvard University Press.

Garmston, R., and B. Wellman. 1999. *The adaptive school: A sourcebook for developing collaborative groups.* Norwood, MA: Christopher-Gordon.

Loucks-Horsley, S., N. Love, K. E. Stiles, S. Mundry, and P. Hewson. 2003. *Designing professional development for teachers of science and mathematics*, 2nd ed. Thousand Oaks, CA: Corwin Press.

Morrissey, M. 2000. *Professional learning communities: An ongoing exploration.* Austin, TX: Southwest Educational Development Laboratory.

National Research Council (NRC). 2007. *Taking science to school.* Washington, DC: National Academies Press.

Piburn, M., and D. Sawada. 2000. *Reformed teaching observational protocol: Reference manual.* ACEPT Technical Report IN00-3. Tempe: Arizona State University.

Schulman, L. S. 1986. Those who understand: Knowledge growth in teaching. *Educational Researcher* 15 (2): 4–14.

Weiss, I. R. 1999. *Evaluating mathematics and science professional development programs.* Chapel Hill, NC: Horizon Research Inc.

Weiss, I. R., J. D. Pasley, P. S. Smith, E. R. Banilower, and D. J. Heck. 2003. *Looking inside the classroom: A study of K–12 mathematics and science education in the United States.* Chapel Hill, NC: Horizon Research Inc.

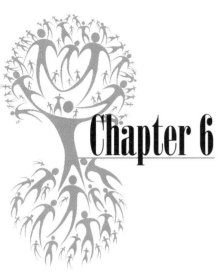

Chapter 6

Attributes of Content-Focused Professional Learning Communities That Lead to Meaningful Reflection and Collaboration Among Math and Science Teachers

Michael Oehrtman, Marilyn Carlson, and Jo Anne Vasquez

"Isolation buffers mediocrity and hides high performers from those who might learn from their modeling, consultation, and coaching. When practice is deprivatized, teachers visit one another's classrooms to observe master teaching, to coach each other, to mentor, and to problem solve in the living laboratory of instructional space."

—Robert Garmston and Bruce Wellman, *The Adaptive School* (1999, p.18)

Chapter 6

Teaching reform efforts in the United States have often shown only short-term effects. Based on an analysis of video data from the Third International Mathematics and Science Study (TIMSS), Stigler and Hiebert (1999) argued that the reason for such limited success is that teaching is embedded in cultural practices whose pervasiveness is too great to overcome through standard professional development activities. They further argued that real change in school culture requires that teachers engage in career-long learning.

Long-term collaboration among teachers focused on student thinking and classroom practices is the basis of the successful and widely lauded practice of Japanese lesson study (Ma 1999; Shimizu 2002; Stigler and Hiebert 1999; Yoshida 1999). Pointing to the Japanese model, Stigler and Hiebert illustrated how teachers can collaborate to treat their classrooms as laboratories for developing, evaluating, refining, and disseminating new instructional ideas. Lesson study members plan, implement, and study an actual lesson that is designed to achieve specific learning goals. Researchers commonly assist the teachers in collecting and analyzing videos of the lesson while it is being taught. The results inform further revisions to the lesson, then the lesson is taught again (Fernandez and Chokshi 2002; Lewis 2002b, 2002c; Lewis and Tsuchida 1998).

In addition to lesson study, other collaborative teacher groups have emerged around the country that are examining "records of practice" such as student work and classroom video (Ball and Bass 2002). Supporting the profession of teaching in a long-term scientific endeavor of reflecting on their practice shows significant promise for effecting real improvement in the U.S. education system.

Research suggests that among the best ways for teachers to improve practice is to spend more time not with their students but with their colleagues. According to Newmann and Wehlage (1995), "If schools want to…boost student learning, they should work on building a professional community that is characterized by shared purpose, collaborative activity, and collective responsibility among staff" (p. 37). The National Partnership for Excellence and Accountability in Teaching (Cibulka 2000) further suggested that teachers are more likely to change when they feel involved and supported in a collegial community of learners.

Regardless of the specific approach, all of these learning communities have in common involvement of groups of teachers to examine actual classroom data, determine what aspects of lessons have been effective, and incorporate subsequent revisions into their instruction. Although participating teachers typically express having a very positive experience, questions have been raised about how to ensure a high-quality conversation based on a deep understanding of the content (Lewis 2002a; Ma 1999). When observing a group of U.S. and Japanese elementary school teachers engaged in lesson study, Fernandez, Cannon, and Chokshi (2003) found that "the Japanese teachers displayed both a strong interest and remarkable insights into the development of content within a lesson. This was in sharp contrast to the American teachers who often did not think about these issues or, when prompted by their Japanese peers, lacked depth in explaining the content" (p. 178). Ma (1999) showed that shallow subject knowledge restricts teachers' capacity to promote conceptual learning among students. Catherine Lewis (2002c) noted that "lesson study alone does not ensure access to content knowledge" (p. 31). Findings such as these suggest that deep content knowledge should not be an assumed benefit of a learning community; rather, it is a goal that must be actively targeted in the community planning and implementation.

DuFour and Eaker (1998) defined highly effective teacher collaborations as ones in which teachers gain conceptual and pedagogical knowledge and transfer that knowledge into observable and quantifiable improvements in their classroom practices. One approach for supporting the content focus of such effective collaborations is to have teachers explore challenging content, scientific inquiry, and problem solving in teams (LaChance and Confrey 2003; Westheimer and Kahne 1993). Unfortunately, American teachers have little opportunity for the types of *meaningful collaboration* with their peers as in efforts described above. By "meaningful," we emphasize the need for long-term, scientific engagement of issues of teaching and learning, such as that made possible by the Japanese lesson study model. We emphasize "collaboration" as one of the most essential goals for these communities to open teachers' classroom doors to the "critical colleagueship" of their peers (Lord 1994).

Recent moves by school districts in Arizona to provide scheduled time and resources for teachers to organize into small groups called professional learning communities (PLCs) have presented an opportunity to study effective practices and crucial support systems for establishing PLCs that engage in meaningful collaboration about their practice. After five years of developing and investigating PLCs in local schools, we have uncovered attributes that differentiate high-performing PLCs from lower-performing PLCs and have begun to uncover critical features for supporting and evaluating PLCs (Carlson et al. 2008). Our research has also identified detrimental beliefs about learning and teaching that can prevent teachers from translating positive experiences in PLCs into their own practice.

Background

Project Pathways is a Math and Science Partnership Program at Arizona State University supported by the National Science Foundation to implement and research teacher professional development in six large urban school districts in Arizona. Teams of STEM (science, technology, engineering, and mathematics) faculty, STEM education faculty, and secondary teachers partnered to create four graduate-level courses for secondary teachers. The courses were designed to support teachers in constructing deep understandings and connections of key STEM ideas and

processes and engage teachers in authentic tasks that foster genuine inquiry about what is involved in knowing, learning, and teaching ideas in math and science and that support developing the habits of mind of a scientific thinker. A critical component of Project Pathways has been school-based PLCs for interdisciplinary groups of secondary mathematics and science teachers. PLC sessions engage teachers in

- conceptual conversations about knowing and learning central ideas in secondary mathematics and science;
- discussion and assessment of student thinking;
- development of inquiry-based, conceptually focused lessons; and
- meaningful reflection on the effectiveness of their instruction.

Focus on Content

The 1998 National Science Foundation report *Shaping the Future* calls for universities to channel more professional development support to the nation's teachers, especially to deepen their content knowledge. Far from having the "profound understanding" of content that characterizes effective teachers (Ma 1999), American teachers often have a shallow understanding of concepts and the connections among concepts that reveal STEM subjects as internally logical and coherent systems of knowledge and practice (Ball 1996; Cooney and Wilson 1993; Monk 1994; Norman 1992). This shallow understanding forces teachers to fall back on "stand and deliver" styles of teaching that emphasize rote memorization and calculational procedures. Rarely do American teachers engage students in deep-thinking explorations that develop critical minds capable of understanding challenging mathematical and scientific concepts (Stigler and Hiebert 1999). In a high-minority-population state like Arizona, superficial teaching of STEM subjects is especially damaging, because it disproportionately undermines the learning of minority and low-income students (Borman, Stringfield, and Rachuba 2000; Wenglinsky 1998).

Project Pathways courses and workshops have undergone three iterations of refinement and are now effective in promoting shifts in teachers' content knowledge for teaching precalculus-level mathematics and central ideas of physics, chemistry, geology, biology, and engineering. We use the Precalculus Concept Assessment (PCA) to assess foundational understandings and reasoning behaviors needed for success in beginning calculus and entry-level courses in science and engineering (Carlson, Oehrtman, and Engelke 2008). Although concepts assessed by the PCA provided a unifying thread through all courses and workshops, we also used discipline-specific instruments such as the Force Concept Inventory (Hestenes, Wells, and Swackhamer 1992) and the Geoscience Concept Inventory (Libarkin and Anderson 2005). The research findings have confirmed our hypothesis that translating this new knowledge to an individual's teaching practice requires more than just new understanding of the mathematics or science they teach. It also requires opportunities for teachers to engage in meaningful collaboration about knowing, learning, and teaching mathematics and science, including time and support to redesign, study, and revise new curriculum sequences for selected topics.

The Intervention

The structure of Project Pathways offers an opportunity for high school math and science teachers to work as teams in a collaborative culture of professional development both as students in Project Pathways courses and as teachers in PLCs. In doing so, teachers from STEM disciplines experience modeling of quality inquiry-based math and science pedagogy, not only by the course instructional leaders, but also by their own team members. Although the nature of math-science integration and implementation of enhanced knowledge, understanding, and skills differs in math and science classroom practice, teachers acquire an underlying understanding of the complementary nature of mathematics and science implicit in the pedagogy modeled in the project's courses. In particular, mathematical problem solving, the scientific method, and engineering design all involve the following processes:

- observing and orienting oneself to the nature, elements, and structure of a situation;
- generating hypotheses or potential solution paths through analogical reasoning and rapid mental evaluation;
- conducting selected tests or implementing strategies; and
- evaluating effectiveness and reiterating the process if necessary.

This linkage and integration of mathematics and science has the potential for synergistic impact on student learning in both subjects. The project's four courses facilitate the connections between mathematics, science, and engineering by highlighting these general processes in the teachers' own reasoning as they learn new content, then asking them to apply the same scientific reasoning to issues of student thinking and to their teaching practices. The accompanying PLCs support teachers in revising their own teaching practices and evaluating the outcomes in a scientific manner.

Embedded in the four Project Pathways courses are the project's primary focus areas:

- creating a sustainable culture of collaboration of math and science teachers in PLCs;
- improving teachers' content knowledge for teaching secondary mathematics and science, including a focus on ideas of rate of change, growth patterns in covarying quantities, and mathematical functions for modeling phenomena;

- improving teachers' scientific reasoning, engineering design, and mathematical problem-solving abilities;
- improving teachers' ability to see content connections in secondary mathematics and science and to adapt curriculum to promote these connections in their classrooms; and
- improving teachers' ability to reflect on the quality of their curriculum in relation to student learning.

The Pathways Courses

The four primary courses developed for Project Pathways are Functions and Modeling; Connecting Physics, Chemistry and Mathematics; Connecting Biology, Geology and Mathematics; and Connecting Engineering, Science and Mathematics. Science and math teachers at each school completed the courses together in their own schools in cohorts with no more than 30 members. Each course ran for 15 weeks during the academic year and was provided tuition-free. The partner schools requested that classes meet weekly during the semester, with each course having at least 60 contact hours between faculty and teachers (45 hours in course work and 15 hours in learning communities). The instruction in the courses promoted inquiry and meaning making to encourage participating teachers to adopt this focus in their own instruction with secondary students. The curriculum for all four courses promoted use of STEM behaviors and the ability to draw on and use the concept of function as a mathematical tool in scientific investigations and engineering design.

Course and PLC Norms

During each course, the instructor (a university faculty member) modeled and promoted *speaking with meaning*, a way of communicating that was negotiated as a goal during the first day of the course. In light of previous observations that revealed poor-quality discourse during the class and the PLCs, the instructor held a class discussion on "rules of engagement" that would be beneficial to improve communication and promote teacher development during the course and the PLC sessions. The notion of speaking with meaning conveyed that teachers would attempt to speak so that their words carry meaning to the listener, and are thus conceptually based; be specific by referencing quantities and avoiding the use of vague pronouns in explanations when appropriate; and explain and justify solution approaches so that the rationale for the approach can be understood by others. The rules of engagement also included such guidelines as exhibiting intellectual integrity (e.g., basing conjectures on logic, not pretending to understand when one doesn't really understand), respecting the learning process of colleagues, and attempting to make sense of colleague's meanings. Investigations revealed that the facilitators in cohort 1 had difficulty modeling and reinforcing these behaviors. This led to our developing facilitator workshops designed to support the facilitators in modeling speaking with meaning and promoting meaningful communication among members of a PLC.

The PLC Facilitator and PLC Sessions

Each PLC had an assigned peer leader who was charged with facilitating discussions during the PLC meetings. The facilitators were selected based on their leadership abilities as recommended by their district math/science coordinator and were initially trained during four 6-hour summer workshops. In addition to the weekly meetings, the facilitators also attended three 3-hour workshops during the semester. These workshops focused on developing specific attributes for facilitation that included the ability to ask questions to promote conceptual explanations and conversations. They were also supported in improving their facilitation ability during weekly coaching sessions with project staff. The workshop leaders engaged the PLC facilitators in a series of activities designed to improve their abilities to both listen to the quality of mathematical and scientific explanations with respect to their conceptual nature and learn to pose questions that promote reflection on what is involved in understanding, learning, and teaching specific science and mathematics concepts. For instance, one activity included viewing and discussing videos of students as they explained their thinking when responding to conceptual tasks. This activity asked the facilitators to discuss what they could infer about student understandings from the video and their rationale behind these inferences.

Senior project personnel led weekly facilitator coaching sessions with the facilitators. During each coaching session, the coach asked questions about the facilitation behaviors observed in the video of each facilitator during their previous PLC sessions to promote reflection about the quality of various PLC interactions. As the coach viewed these videos with the research team before the coaching meetings, they discussed the facilitators' effectiveness in promoting and enacting speaking with meaning about issues of knowing, learning, and teaching the content that was the focus of that PLC agenda. These discussions provided opportunities for the coach to address specific interactions during the coaching meetings that either promoted or inhibited meaningful discourse among members of a PLC.

The coach's strategies for promoting reflection about PLC interactions progressed from general discussions to making specific prompts to each PLC facilitator. During the first few coaching sessions, the coach discussed positive moves that she and the research team were noticing in hopes that the PLC facilitators who were less effective would begin to adopt the more effective strategies. As one example, she noted that when PLC members appeared to be speaking past each other, the facilitator of the PLC prompted the PLC members to put a written product on

Chapter 6

the whiteboard and encouraged the PLC members to speak about the ideas of the problem. The facilitator coach also gave general suggestions that she thought might promote positive facilitator moves, such as making an effort to listen to the meanings that the PLC members were communicating and trying to ask questions based on these meanings. As the PLC coach sensed that the facilitators were becoming more comfortable in their role as a facilitator, she became more direct with each of the PLC facilitators about behaviors that were less effective.

Results of Research on Project Pathways PLCs

The professional development implementation and the research design for Project Pathways was guided by previous research studies that investigated and articulated the process of learning, understanding, and using the concept of function (Carlson 1998; Oehrtman, Carlson, and Thompson 2008) and attending to the covarying patterns in phenomena (Carlson et al. 2002). Three discipline-specific frameworks that articulate the processes of STEM inquiry (Atman et al. 2007; Carlson and Bloom 2005; Lawson 2001) informed the development of course modules and classroom instruction and served as lenses for analyzing discourse patterns in the course and PLCs.

Teachers and district leaders in the Project Pathways partnership overwhelmingly cited their participation in these PLCs as the most rewarding and effective component of the project. Pathways research teams have generated extensive data corroborating these anecdotal claims and have uncovered critical variables that affect the functioning of these PLCs. We have identified crucial components of PLC formation and support that lead to inquiry and engagement about issues of student thinking and learning. Our analysis of qualitative data on teachers' engagement in their PLCs resulted in the emergence of three central categories of *process behaviors* generalizing the discipline-specific frameworks for STEM inquiry and three categories of *dispositional behaviors* related to their approach to discourse. We have also observed that the PLC facilitator is a key variable in promoting meaningful discourse among the PLC members.

Process Behaviors of PLC Members

Analysis of video data from PLC sessions revealed specific behaviors and dispositions of the PLC members that led to quality discourse about knowing, learning, and teaching mathematics and science. The three general process behaviors are productive engagement, effective use of conceptual resources, and persistence and reflection.

- *Productive engagement* is characterized by the PLC members exploring or clarifying some issue that is problematic to the PLC members, and all members of the PLC are encouraged to participate.

- *Effective use of conceptual resources* is characterized by the PLC members intentionally seeking and selecting relevant concepts or ideas to advance their discussions. The PLC members are alert to the possibility that they may have gaps in their collective understanding and may need to seek information from print or online resources or individuals not in the PLC.
- *Persistence and reflection* implies that the PLC members stay engaged until a problem is resolved; this is followed by their evaluating the quality of their solution and reflecting on the effectiveness of the tools they applied.

Table 6.1 provides productive and unproductive examples of these PLC process behaviors.

Table 6.1. Process Behaviors

Category	Productive Examples	Unproductive Examples
Productive engagement	Members engage in exploring a common problematic issue, clarify the nature of the problem, and encourage participation of all members.	Members work routinely through the agenda without reflective engagement, are not focused on a common issue, and exclude others from participating.
Conceptual resources	Members are intentional in their selection of conceptual resources to apply to a problem, apply appropriate and powerful ideas, and seek appropriate external assistance when there is a gap in their collective understanding.	Members choose inappropriate content-based tools, are not able to properly apply tools appropriately, and regularly offer irrelevant or incorrect statements.
Persistence and reflection	Members stay engaged until a problem is resolved, evaluate the quality of their solution, and reflect on the effectiveness of the tools they applied.	Members offer suggestions and ideas without evaluation of appropriateness, are satisfied with solutions without understanding, and quickly give up when they are not successful.

Dispositional Behaviors of PLC Members

Our study of the communication patterns of the PLCs revealed that the initial level of discourse and the quality of the communication were not very high. Members of the PLCs were often focused on performing procedures, and their explanations often focused on these procedures as opposed to the underlying concepts of the problem (see Table 6.2). We observed that conversations between two PLC members often did not result in an exchange of ideas, and the teachers were observed talking past each other with little discussion of student learning and what is involved in understanding mathematics and science concepts.

As the semester progressed, teachers' attempts to speak with meaning emerged as a stronger social norm. During PLC sessions, the teachers began attempting to justify their responses with more than just procedural explanations. In these cases, the members often used the context of the problem in their explanations and made observable attempts to provide a rationale for their approach; however, their explanations were often insufficient in that they did not include a coherent justification for their solution approach.

Table 6.2. Dispositional Behaviors

Category	Productive Examples	Unproductive Examples
Conceptual orientation	Members clarify ideas, focus on meanings in mathematical and scientific activity, and identify and resolve ambiguity.	Members focus on procedures without connection to meaning, offer answers as sole evidence of student understanding, and use jargon without clarification.
Intellectual integrity	Members provide rationale for claims, exhibit honesty about lack of understanding, and show willingness to challenge others and be challenged.	Members avoid putting their thinking on the table, defer to authority, and avoid confronting each other on incorrect or inconsistent statements.
Coherence	Members seek and establish connections among ideas and topics, express ideas using multiple representations, and generalize conclusions to other settings or find limiting conditions.	Members treat concepts as isolated and unrelated, fixate on single ideas, and are not open to other solutions.

As PLC facilitators further fostered the emergence of the social norms for what would constitute a sufficient explanation or justification, teachers began to hold each other accountable for providing more meaningful explanations, and hence establish criteria for speaking with meaning. Over the course of the semester, they began demanding that justifications be conceptual and that individuals include a clear articulation of the quantities, relationships, and implications inherent in the problem or context under discussion.

Beliefs and Attitudes

Use of quantitative instruments, such as the Views About Mathematics Survey (VAMS; Carlson 1997) and the Views About Science Survey (VASS; Halloun 1997; Halloun and Hestenes 1998), revealed shortcomings in teachers' views about the methods of doing mathematics and science that informed our refinement of the course. However, early in the project we discovered that these instruments did not sufficiently account for many of the key objectives of the project (especially related to the integration of STEM disciplines) and perceived barriers to implementing reform that were exhibited by the teachers. In our analysis of video data, the coding of these beliefs converged around four categories as outlined in Table 6.3: factors of resistance, beliefs about STEM learning, beliefs about STEM teaching, and confidence and perceived ability in STEM disciplines.

Decentering and Facilitator Strategies

Tracking the facilitation abilities of PLC facilitators revealed interaction patterns between the facilitator and other PLC members that influenced the quality of inquiry among the group. Our analyses also revealed that the degree to which the facilitator was willing and able to build models of other members' thinking when interacting with them influenced the meaningfulness of the exchange. We found

Table 6.3. Categories of Belief

Category	Examples
Factors of resistance	"The pace at which I must cover material does not allow me to teach ideas deeply." "My school administrators do not value my efforts to get students to understand ideas deeply."
Beliefs about STEM learning	"Making unsuccessful attempts when working on a mathematics problem is an indication of one's weakness in mathematics." "Learning happens when students are provided opportunities to construct meaning and make connections."
Beliefs about STEM teaching	"It is important to understand what a student is thinking when s/he asks a question." "The primary goal of my exams is to assess if my students can memorize facts and carry out procedures like ones required for completing the homework."
Confidence and perceived ability in STEM disciplines	"I feel prepared to create learning opportunities for my students that promote connections between mathematics and science." "I have a clear understanding of how central ideas of my courses develop in students."

Note: STEM = science, technology, engineering, and mathematics.

that most facilitators gradually improved in both of these abilities as a result of coaching by project personnel.

To actively facilitate teachers in a PLC requires that the facilitator "place" her- or himself in the other members' shoes. Placing oneself in another's shoes is a classic example of what Piaget (1955) identified as *decentering*, or the attempt to adopt a perspective that is not one's own. Steffe and Thompson (2000) extended Piaget's idea of decentering to the case of interactions between teacher and student (or mentor and protégé) by distinguishing between ways in which one person attempts to systematically influence another. In that process, each person acts as an observer of the other, creating models of the other's ways of thinking.

The construct of decentering implies that it is important for a facilitator to both remain attentive to the fact that each member of the group has a rationality that is completely her or his own and attempt to discern that rationality. The activity of decentering is important to a PLC setting, but it is also applicable to a classroom. If one is truly concerned with student learning, it is necessary to build models of students' thinking and base further interactions on these models. Analysis of the facilitators revealed four observable manifestations of decentering, with a fifth manifestation hypothesized from our theoretical perspective (Table 6.4).

We observed that the facilitator decentering moves that had the greatest implications for the quality of the PLC discourse occurred while modeling or encouraging productive process and dispositional behaviors as outlined earlier in this chapter. Examples of the effective facilitator strategies we observed are provided in Table 6.5.

Chapter 6

Table 6.4. Facilitator Decentering Moves (FDMs) in a Professional Learning Community (PLC)

Code	Facilitator Action
FDM 1	The facilitator shows no interest in understanding the thinking or perspective of a PLC member with whom he/she is interacting.
FDM 2	The facilitator takes actions to model a PLC member's thinking, but does not use that model in communication with the PLC member.
FDM 3	The facilitator builds a model of a PLC member's thinking and recognizes that it is different from his/her own. The facilitator then acts in ways to move the PLC member to his/her way of thinking, but does so in a manner that does not build on the rationale of the other member.
FDM 4	The facilitator builds a model of a PLC member's thinking and acts in ways that respect and build on the rationality of this member's thinking for the purpose of advancing the PLC member's thinking and/or understanding.
FDM 5	The facilitator builds a model of a PLC member's thinking and respects that it has a rationality of its own. Through interaction, the facilitator also builds a model of how he/she is being interpreted by the PLC member. He/she then adjusts his/her actions (questions, drawings, statements) to take into account both the PLC member's thinking and how the facilitator might be interpreted by that PLC member.

Both the science and math facilitators initially showed little tendency to decenter. At the beginning of the course and in their early PLC sessions they frequently expressed that they were accustomed to viewing teaching as carrying out procedures or explaining how to get answers to specific types of problems. Both their direct comments and discussions when completing tasks revealed that they were uncomfortable participating in professional development that focused on making meaning of science and mathematics ideas. They often expressed some frustration in being asked to reason and explain their thinking about fundamental ideas such as force, pressure, and rate of change. However, as the course and PLC sessions progressed they began to express appreciation of efforts to hold them accountable for thinking deeply about the processes and connections needed to understand and use central ideas in the curriculum that they teach.

Table 6.5. Facilitator Strategies

Examples of Strategies for Fostering Process Behaviors

- *Productive engagement:* Facilitator asks questions to cause disequilibrium about an important topic, focus all participants on a common issue, and encourage reflection.
- *Conceptual resources:* Facilitator possesses and directs the use of appropriate content and pedagogical tools or manages the discussion to capitalize on the expertise of each member.
- *Persistence and reflection:* Facilitator encourages the members to evaluate their solutions and assess whether they have made their reasoning clear to the group.

Examples of Strategies for Fostering Dispositional Behaviors

- *Conceptual orientation:* Facilitator refocuses discussions about how to "do" problems toward the meanings of quantities and procedures, and requests and models speaking meaningfully.
- *Intellectual integrity:* Facilitator asks members to provide rationale for their thinking, points out inconsistencies, and checks with members about what they do and do not understand.
- *Coherence:* Facilitator asks for multiple representations and guides the discourse in the group to compare and extend ideas and consider subtleties, exceptions, and alternative explanations.

National Science Teachers Association

Through the facilitator workshops and coaching, most of the facilitators improved their ability to decenter over the course of the year. These facilitators appeared to value efforts to understand others' thinking and be motivated to engage in discourse to uncover meaning of the ideas under discussion. As their ability to decenter improved, their questioning improved and the quality of the discourse among members of the PLC became more meaningful.

Even for facilitators with weak mathematical or scientific backgrounds, the discussions in their PLCs became more meaningful over the year, although these improvements did not result from the facilitators decentering during interactions with their colleagues. In fact, weak mathematical or scientific understandings, as revealed by classroom and performance data, appeared to limit their ability to decenter in the context of discussions about mathematical and scientific ideas. Analysis of video data from these PLCs revealed that making strategic moves would enhance a mathematically or scientifically weak facilitator's effectiveness. For example, the facilitator might ask questions that promote reflection and decentering by other members of the PLC, as they are encouraged to interact with each other. The quality of the exchanges that followed such moves to facilitate discussions among the PLC members appeared to be affected by the decentering abilities and depth of mathematical and scientific understanding of other members of the PLC. Thus, although a mathematically or scientifically weak facilitator may not be able to understand or follow all discussions, he or she may still be effective by posing general questions to engage members of the PLC in making meaning of ideas and others' thinking.

The Role of the District and School Administrators

The support of participating school principals and math and science department chairs has been critical for sustaining Project Pathways interventions. Since cohort 3 had at most 40% of the math and science teachers from a given school, we anticipated obstacles to scaling up the PLCs to all teachers within a school, and as interest emerged among teachers to scale up Pathways interventions within a school, we met some resistance. As one example, 8 of 31 math and science teachers from a particular school became highly motivated to institutionalize the PLCs so that they could continue them at their school with all of their colleagues participating. Pathways project leadership met with the school principal, the math department chair, and the science department chair, and although there was initial interest, the math department chair later determined that it would be logistically difficult to arrange teacher schedules so that PLCs could meet during the school day. He also revealed that he thought Pathways was only needed for younger teachers in his department. His resistance led to the school discontinuing PLC meetings and their choosing to not have the project offer courses or workshops to other teachers in the school.

This situation may have been avoided had we required that prior to infusing funds in a particular school the principal agree to scale up interventions that were valued by a majority of the teachers.

After this event, the project Principal Investigator (PI) contacted the project's funder to request permission to select a few Pathways schools for cohort 4. The goal was to begin cohort 4 intervention with a school in which the principal, math department chair, and science department chair were all supportive of Pathways courses and PLCs. In negotiating strategies with the principal for obtaining 100% participation from the math and science teachers in his school, we determined that not all teachers were able to enroll in the graduate course sequence. This resulted in our deciding to hold monthly three-hour workshops, with similar content focus as the courses, for teachers who were unwilling or unable to participate in the full course. The project PI also met with the superintendent and other district curriculum administrators to discuss Pathways goals and to communicate to them what school and district commitments would be needed to adopt that school as a Pathways-designated school. The response and support from these administrators resulted in them doing the following:

- agreeing to rearrange the school schedule so that content-focused PLCs could meet for one hour each week during the school day,
- agreeing to pay PLC facilitators an extra stipend and to pay all teachers for their time in participating in Pathways PLCs, and
- hiring substitutes so that teachers not enrolled in the course could participate in the monthly workshops during the school day.

We are about one semester into the intervention for this cohort and are appreciative of the support we are receiving from the principal of this school. He expressed to the project PI that he has been visiting his teachers' classes and is already seeing a difference in the level of student engagement and focus on teaching relevant ideas in classrooms in his school.

Summary

Transforming the professional development culture and teaching practices of science and mathematics teachers within a school requires sustained efforts and a supportive school environment. Courses or experiences that engage teachers in inquiry and improve teachers' understanding of the content they teach are a critical variable for the transformation of teaching practices. Shifts in teachers' *content knowledge for teaching* enables them to examine student thinking and develop meaningful lessons for students. However, local factors (e.g., district or departmental exams, the school curriculum) often present obstacles that must be navigated as teachers work to improve their teaching practice.

A facilitator who listens to the meanings of other PLC members and subsequently probes and promotes reflection and meaning making can have a positive impact on the quality of the discourse in a PLC. Promoting genuine inquiry about issues of knowing, learning, or teaching are productive to the extent that the facilitator and other PLC members possess the conceptual tools and habits of persisting and reflecting. PLCs that have members who strive for coherence and connections and spontaneously provide a rationale for claims are also more likely to exhibit quality discourse about teaching and learning. When starting PLCs within a school, it is important to select PLC facilitators who value these process and dispositional behaviors. Initial workshops that support PLC facilitators in attending to the thinking and learning of their colleagues can also substantially increase the effectiveness of a PLC facilitator.

Reflection Questions

- To what extent do math and science teachers in your context currently interact? If you plan to integrate math and science PLCs, what benefits do you expect teachers to gain from interdisciplinary collaboration? How might the Pathways perspective of inquiry as a generalization of mathematical problem solving, scientific inquiry, and engineering design be employed in your context?

- What lessons can you draw from the Pathways implementation to help teachers see student thinking and their own teaching practices as problematic and worthy of inquiry? How can you support teachers to make data-driven claims and decisions and evaluate the effectiveness of their actions?

- What expectations for interactions among teachers in PLCs do you find most critical to foster the Pathways vision of meaningful inquiry? What lessons from the Pathways PLCs might help teachers to overcome the intense social pressure to resist challenging each other and to hold each other accountable for speaking with meaning and exhibiting intellectual integrity? How can you ensure the quality of content and pedagogical discourse in the PLCs?

- What pressures do teachers in your context face that may result in resistance to the objectives and practices of productive PLCs? What lessons from the Pathways implementation may help you to confront potentially counterproductive beliefs?

- What options for PLC facilitation exist in your context? What support is necessary to help facilitators decenter and foster productive process and dispositional behaviors in their PLCs?

Chapter 6

References

Atman, C., R. Adams, M. Cardella, J. Turns, S. Mosborg, and J. Saleem. 2007. Engineering design processes: A comparison of students and expert practitioners. *Journal of Engineering Education* 96 (4): 359–379.

Ball, D. L. 1996. Teacher learning and the mathematics reforms: What do we think we know and what do we need to learn? *Phi Delta Kappan* 77 (7): 500–508.

Ball, D., and H. Bass. 2002. Professional development through records of instruction. In *Studying classroom teaching as a medium for professional development: Proceedings of a U.S.–Japan workshop*, eds. H. Bass, Z. P. Usiskin, and G. Burrill, 79–89. Washington, DC: National Academy Press.

Borman, G., S. Stringfield, and L. Rachuba. 2000. *Advancing minority high achievement: National trends and promising programs and practices.* New York: College Board.

Carlson, M. 1997. The development of an instrument to assess students' views about the methods and learnability of mathematics. In *Proceedings of the 19th Annual Meeting of the North American Chapter of the International Group for the Psychology of Mathematics Education, Vol. 2,* eds. J. Dossey, J. Swafford, M. Parmantie, and A. Dossey, 395–403. Columbus: Ohio State University.

Carlson, M. 1998. A cross-sectional investigation of the development of the function concept. In *Research in Collegiate Mathematics Education. III. CBMS Issues in Mathematics Education,* eds. A. H. Schoenfeld, J. Kaput, and E. Dubinsky, 114–163. Providence, RI: American Mathematical Society.

Carlson, M., and I. Bloom. 2005. The cyclic nature of problem solving: An emergent multidimensional problem-solving framework. *Educational Studies in Mathematics* 58: 45–75.

Carlson, M., S. Jacobs, E. Coe, S. Larsen, and E. Hsu. 2002. Applying covariational reasoning while modeling dynamic events: A framework and a study. *Journal for Research in Mathematics Education* 33: 352–378.

Carlson, M., M. Oehrtman, and N. Engelke. 2008. The precalculus concept assessment (PCA) instrument: A tool for assessing reasoning patterns, understandings and knowledge of precalculus level students. (Unpublished manuscript under review)

Carlson, M., M. Oehrtman, S. Bowling, and K. Moore. 2008. The emergence of decentering in facilitators of professional learning communities of secondary mathematics and science teachers. (Unpublished manuscript under review)

Cibulka, J. 2000. *Practitioners' guide to learning communities. The creation of high-performance schools through organizational learning.* RFP-97-0101, Project 4.4.1. Washington, DC: National Partnership for Excellence and Accountability in Teaching.

Cooney, T., and M. Wilson. 1993. Teachers' thinking about functions: Historical and research perspectives. In *Integrating research on the graphical representation of functions*, eds. T. A. Romberg, E. Fennema, and T. P. Carpenter, 131–138. Hillsdale, NJ: Lawrence Erlbaum.

DuFour, R., and R. Eaker. 1998. *Professional learning communities at work: Best practices for enhancing student achievement.* Bloomington, IN: National Educational Service.

Fernandez, C., and S. Chokshi. 2002. A practical guide to translating lesson study for a U.S. setting. *Phi Delta Kappan* 84 (2): 128–134.

Fernandez, C., J. Cannon, and S. Chokshi. 2003. A U.S.–Japan lesson study collaboration reveals critical lenses for examining practice. *Teaching and Teacher Education* 19 (2): 171–185.

Garmston, R. J., and B. M. Wellman. 1999. *The adaptive school: A sourcebook for developing collaborative groups.* Norwood, MA: Christopher-Gordon.

Halloun, I. 1997. Views about science and physics achievement: The VASS story. In *The changing role of physics departments in modern universities: Proceedings of ICUPE*, eds. E. Redish and J. Rigden, 605–614. College Park, MD: American Institute of Physics Press.

Halloun, I., and D. Hestenes. 1998. Interpreting VASS dimensions and profiles. *Science and Education* 7(6): 553–577.

Hestenes, D., M. Wells, and G. Swackhamer. 1992. Force Concept Inventory. *The Physics Teacher* 30: 141–158.

LaChance, A., and J. Confrey. 2003. Interconnecting content and community: A qualitative study of secondary mathematics teachers. *Journal of Mathematics Teacher Education* 6: 107–137.

Lawson, A. E. 2001. Using the learning cycle to teach biology concepts and reasoning patterns. *Journal of Biological Education* 35 (4): 165–169.

Lewis, C. 2002a. Does lesson study have a future in the United States? *Journal of Education and Human Development* 1: 1–23.

Lewis, C. 2002b. *Lesson study: A handbook of teacher-led instructional change.* Philadelphia: Research for Better Schools.

Lewis, C. 2002c. What are the essential elements of lesson study? *California Science Project Connection* 2 (6): 1–4.

Lewis, C., and I. Tsuchida. 1998. A lesson is like a swiftly flowing river: Research lessons and the improvement of Japanese education. *American Educator* (Winter): 14–17, 50–52.

Libarkin, J. C., and S. W. Anderson. 2005. Assessment of learning in entry-level geoscience courses: Results from the Geoscience Concept Inventory. *Journal of Geoscience Education* 53: 394–401.

Lord, B. 1994. Teachers' professional development: Critical colleagueship and the role of professional community. In *The future of education: Perspectives*

Chapter 6

on national standards in America, ed. N. Cobb, 175–204. New York: College Entrance Examination Board.

Ma, L. 1999. *Knowing and teaching elementary mathematics*. Mahwah, NJ: Lawrence Erlbaum.

Monk, D. H. 1994. Subject area preparation of secondary mathematics and science teachers and student achievement. *Economics of Education Review* 13 (2): 125–145.

National Science Foundation (NSF), Committee for the Review of Undergraduate Education. 1998. *Shaping the future: New expectations for undergraduate education in science, mathematics, engineering, and technology*. Arlington, VA: NSTA.

Newmann, F. M., and G. G. Wehlage. 1995. *Successful school restructuring: A report to the public and educators*. Madison, WI: Center on Organization and Restructuring of Schools. (ERIC Document Reproduction Service no. ED387925)

Norman, A. 1992. Teachers' mathematical knowledge of the concept of function. In *The concept of function: Aspects of epistemology and pedagogy*, eds. G. Harel and E. Dubinsky, 215–232. MAA Notes Vol. 25.

Oehrtman, M., M. Carlson, and P. W. Thompson. 2008. Foundational reasoning abilities that promote coherence in students' function understanding. In *Making the connection: Research and practice in undergraduate mathematics*, eds. M. Carlson and C. Rasmussen, 27–41. MAA Notes Vol. 73. Washington, DC: Mathematical Association of America.

Piaget, J. 1955. *The language and thought of the child*. New York: Meridian Books.

Shimizu, Y. 2002. Lesson study: What, why, and how? In *Studying classroom teaching as a medium for professional development: Proceedings of a U.S.–Japan workshop*, eds. H. Bass, Z. P. Usiskin, and G. Burrill, 53–57. Washington, DC: National Academy Press.

Steffe, L. P., and P. W. Thompson. 2000. Interaction or intersubjectivity? A reply to Lerman. *Journal for Research in Mathematics Education* 31 (2): 191–209.

Stigler, J., and J. Hiebert. 1999. *The teaching gap: Best ideas from the world's teachers for improving education in the classroom*. New York: Free Press.

Wenglinsky, H. 1998. *Does it compute? The relationship between educational technology and student achievement in mathematics*. Princeton, NJ: Educational Testing Service.

Westheimer, J., and J. Kahne. 1993. Building school communities: An experience-based model. *Phi Delta Kappan* 75 (4): 324–328.

Yoshida, M. 1999. Lesson study [Jugyokenkyu] in elementary school mathematics in Japan: A case study. Paper presented at the annual meeting of the American Educational Research Association, Montreal.

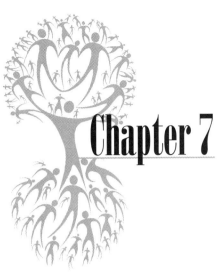

Chapter 7

The Role of Local and State Science Leaders in Developing Professional Learning Communities

Gregory MacDougall

Are two heads better than one?

Chapter 7

This chapter begins with this question for two reasons. First, think to yourself how many times it was helpful to collaborate with other people on a project, especially when undertaking complex, challenging work. Second, the question reflects the idea that the pursuit of finding answers, sometimes to a simple question, unites professionals in a process of collective inquiry. Promoting collaboration and collective inquiry is at the heart of professional learning communities (PLCs). This chapter tells two stories, both focused on the role of science leadership in developing the teacher leadership that is essential for creating and maintaining PLCs, where "many heads are better than one." The first story provides insight into how district leaders systematically created the teacher leadership and support needed for a PLC to form in one school district. The second is a vignette of a statewide initiative in South Carolina that is building teacher leadership to support PLCs in schools.

There is ample literature on the principal's role in creating and maintaining a PLC. Although the role of the principal is critical to changing school culture, two other roles are often overlooked. Science leadership and teacher leaders in the school must be actively engaged and supported to lead science-focused PLCs. In effective PLCs, teacher leaders bring fellow colleagues together in a collaborative environment to inquire into ways of improving student learning. This collaborative work environment is often counter to the culture of the school and is not part of the usual professional development (Usdan, McCloud, and Podmostko 2001). In order to provide teacher leaders with the knowledge and skills to impact the culture of schools, it is imperative that they engage in high-quality professional development and support, not only on the concept of PLCs, but also on the change process, instructional best practices, coaching and facilitation skills, and science content.

This chapter presents examples of the role of science leadership at the school, district, and state levels in providing professional development and support of teacher leaders in schools to develop effective PLCs. The chapter provides examples of teacher leadership development activities and frameworks and illustrates the roles of teacher leaders who help facilitate traditional teacher teams becoming professional learning teams (PLTs) and PLCs. The examples provided in this chapter come from my work as a district science coordinator, state science specialist, and member of a state affiliate of the National Science Education Leadership Association.

District Support of Teacher Leaders

Between 1982 and 1987 the National Science Teachers Association (NSTA) organized the Search for Excellence in Science Education. During this time, researchers sought to (1) identify highly successful science education programs, (2) investigate the characteristics of the programs, (3) share that information with the nation, and (4) influence systemic change in the form of a series of policy statements from NSTA. As a result of this initiative, 17 articles were published that investigated exemplary science education programs. These programs covered K–16 education, including schools of education. This work would later inspire my own search for best practices.

I became a high school science coordinator for 11 high schools in 1998, just as science end-of-course testing was initiated. As the new coordinator for a large school district, it was not the wealth of knowledge I had accumulated from reading those 17 NSTA articles that fueled my passion for increasing student achievement; rather, it was the inquiry into best practices that I found most fascinating. As the new science coordinator, I wanted to identify high-performing teachers, learn the strategies that they believed led to high student achievement, share those strategies with teachers across the district, and influence systemic change. To accomplish these goals, I needed to identify effective teacher leaders who would facilitate this process effectively and efficiently, and to have them form communities in which teaching professionals would learn ways to continually improve student learning and achievement.

Identifying and Preparing Teacher Leaders

Having access to district-wide data, it was relatively easy for me to create a list of high-performing teachers based on their state end-of-course test scores, but I knew there were other factors that may influence student test scores. Therefore, this list alone was not sufficient for identifying high-performing teachers who were successful with all students and implemented best practices in their classrooms. As I looked closely at the teachers on the initial list, I knew there was a great variety of classroom management and teaching styles represented. In addition, the teachers taught a variety of students, from rural to suburban and from schools with populations of relatively high wealth to those of moderate and high poverty. I began a series of conversations with teachers throughout the district during my regular school visits. I was searching for teachers who used a variety of instructional strategies in the classroom, were successful in teaching a diverse student body, knew their subject matter deeply, and could communicate effectively with peers.

It was important to identify strong teachers who were able to teach science to a wide variety of students and bring teachers together to learn collectively and implement best practices for increased student achievement. I found that many teachers I visited and talked with had an inquisitive nature about how they viewed the classroom. Although they already had a repertoire of impressive strategies, they were constantly searching for ways to improve student achievement. As good as they already were, they wanted to learn more about best practices through reading research and collaborating with their peers. The characteristics I saw in these teachers were the ones I believed were essential for leading and inspiring other teachers to make changes in practice.

The first two teachers identified as potential teacher leaders were highly experienced (more than 15 teaching years) and energetic professionals who knew their subject material and cared deeply about students. This is not to say that other teachers in the district did not care about their students. There was, however, something about these teachers that made their level of care and expectations for *all* students palpable in the classroom. Additionally, these teachers had a depth of content understanding that led them to have a great repertoire of approaches to teaching science concepts, so they never ran out of ways to reach all learners. With two teachers identified, a biology teacher and a chemistry teacher, I formulated a series of informal professional development sessions with them for the purpose of preparing to develop learning communities among science teachers across the district. These sessions were heavily influenced by my own professional development provided through the school district.

The school district had a proactive professional development plan and was heavily influenced by the Malcolm Baldrige process for promoting continuous improvement (i.e., the Baldrige National Quality Program of the National Institute of Standards and Technology; see *www.nist.gov/public_affairs/factsheet/baldfaqs.htm* for information on this program). Top-rated consultants were brought to the district to provide professional development. Between 1998 and 2003, I learned about PLCs from Rick DuFour, the effective use of data in decision making from Mike Schmoker, instructional strategies from Bruce Wellman and Laurie Kagan, and continuous improvement resulting in increased student achievement and reductions in student achievement gaps from Gerald Anderson. However, it was the training on facilitation skills and the total quality management from people like David Langford (2002) that provided me with the critical strategies and tools with which I could envision a community coming together and collaboratively working in an effective manner to enhance science teaching. Two heads are not always better than one if people do not have the strategies to work together. DuFour et al. (2006, p. 89) warn that "coblaboration," not collaboration, is the norm where schools do not change the nature of the conversation that teachers are having. My aim was to provide both the strategies and support for teachers to work together effectively.

Building on the quality of the professional development I experienced through the district professional development, I identified a skill set and created a series of informal and individualized professional development sessions to enhance the teacher leaders' skills and abilities to cultivate a collaborative environment where teachers would feel safe to share, hypothesize, and test ideas in their collaborative approach to improve instruction. The initial facilitation session topics focused on creating a results-oriented agenda, creating a common vision, working with a variety of adults, making decisions, involving and honoring participants, using the plan-do-study-act cycle to improve student learning (Anderson 2000), and effectively communicating ideas with the science coordinator.

With all these ideas coming from various sources, I found that I needed to have an overall framework that coordinated the ideas and encapsulated a vision for improvement.

Framework for School Improvement

Through my learning from nationally recognized experts and identifying best practices from high-performing teachers across the district, I began collecting a variety of best practices in curriculum, assessment, and instruction and identifying components of teacher leadership, such as the ability to facilitate teacher meetings and use dialogue about data. I realized I needed a framework for school improvement that was structured enough to guide the actions of the teacher leaders, yet flexible enough to fit in varied contexts. I developed a framework that would systematically guide the vision and work of the teacher leaders in bringing teachers together in a PLC for the purpose of improving student achievement in biology and chemistry classrooms across the district. The inspiration for this framework initially came to me while reviewing a school plan that was developed by a state External Review Team. In the learning community I hoped to create, however, it was not an external team that would diagnose the school, it would be the school faculty themselves, through collaborative work on curriculum, assessment, and instruction (see Table 7.1).

Table 7.1. Framework for School Improvement

Teacher Leadership		
• Use facilitation and coaching skills to create a professional learning environment among staff. • Compile relevant data for the purpose of focusing resources. • Organize and/or facilitate professional development activities based on needs. • Create and implement school improvement plans that involve administration and all teachers.		
Curriculum	**Assessment**	**Instruction**
• Create team pacing charts that broadly outline the material to be taught for the year. • Unpack standards and write curriculum, unit plans, and/or lesson plans that include aligned resources and specific textbook pages. • Systematically review curriculum/unit/lesson effectiveness.	• Create formative and summative assessments that are aligned to the standards and involve a variety of types and levels. • Systematically review assessments for the purpose of improving student understanding of standards. • Allow multiple opportunities for students to master material.	• Ensure that instruction is aligned to the curriculum through systemic monitoring. • Model exemplary instructional strategies that accelerate learning. • Implement exemplary instruction in content areas (English language arts, math, science, social studies), classroom dynamics, and management.

All of the items in this framework for school improvement are non-negotiable. However, it is up to the members of the PLC to decide when to address each component and how each component is translated into best practice in the classroom. The science teacher leaders used this framework to focus ideas for increasing

student achievement. As teachers and teacher leaders used this framework, it was periodically modified based on new information and the needs of the PLC.

Central to this framework is the role of the teacher leader. The skills that the teacher leader needs to facilitate the PLC process are identified at the top of Table 7.1. John Holton, as coordinator for mathematics and science for South Carolina, once said at a meeting that "the marines don't train one marine at a time, they train to work as a team … but teachers are trained one teacher at a time and not as a team." With this in mind, it is a priority for teacher leaders to use facilitation and coaching skills to work effectively with peers and to be able to bring teachers together as a PLC focused on improving student learning and achievement.

Teacher Leaders Forming Learning Communities

After engaging the biology and chemistry teacher leaders in professional development to enhance their knowledge and abilities as facilitators, I secured district professional development funds to support the teacher leaders and participant teachers to conduct monthly (two-hour) after-school meetings focused on curriculum, assessment, and instructional practices that promoted student achievement. Communication occurred frequently through group e-mail. These structural supports provided a way for the biology and chemistry teachers to begin their collaborative work. As the science coordinator, I supported the process by reviewing "results-oriented" agendas ahead of time as well as reviewing the participants' feedback from each session (Langford 2002).

There were several advantages to this organized approach to instituting time for the teachers to convene and communicate in person and via e-mail. First, there was increased communication among the biology teachers and among the chemistry teachers about effective teaching practices and increased communication between these teachers and the science coordinator. Creating the opportunity for teachers to share their ideas for instructional practices directly resulted in some significant changes in curriculum, assessment practices, classroom instruction, and student achievement.

The following two scenarios demonstrate the results of the teacher leaders developing a community among the biology and chemistry teachers.

Biology Teachers' Development of Instructional Materials

Prior to the formation of the biology PLC, there was very little organized collaboration among teachers in the schools. With voluntary district-wide meetings designed to support collaboration among biology teachers, the teachers began to have multiple and systematic opportunities to share their ideas, successes, and pitfalls with peers across the district. Perhaps more importantly, with a teacher leader facilitating the meetings, the meetings became places in which it was safe for ideas to be discussed, for all participants to be involved in decision-making processes, and for them to work together in new ways focused on effective teaching practice.

After several meetings of the biology PLC, the biology lead teacher approached me with an idea from the group to secure funds for a unit on DNA fingerprinting. Knowing that this was a timely issue, it was aligned to the standards, and the teachers were wholeheartedly in favor of this unit, I secured $3,000 worth of equipment for each school and funds for a group of seven teachers to work for one week during the summer to create a coherent unit plan that could be used by all biology teachers and all students in the district.

The teachers' goal during the summer was to develop a series of coherent lessons that would engage students in activities that moved them from a concrete level of understanding of DNA through actual DNA extraction and then to an application of their understanding of DNA to how DNA fingerprinting is used to identify individuals. The labs needed to be designed so that they would be accessible to all students taking biology. Although the equipment was well suited for advanced biology students, the expectation was that the labs would be required core experiences for all biology students across the district. As such, the teachers needed to create a series of labs that biology teachers could successfully implement in any high school biology classroom.

This was not business as usual. In the past, equipment was most often given to teachers without professional development to support their learning of the content or the implementation of the new materials. In the few cases where professional development was provided, it was led by an "expert." In this case, the teachers came together as a collaborative group to identify and prioritize needs and develop a plan to make sure everyone would have the guidance they needed to use the new instructional materials well.

With clear expectations set by the science coordinator, the biology teacher PLC group, led by the lead teacher, met over several days in the summer to collaboratively work on creating the new DNA investigations. On one day of the sessions, I made a scheduled visit to the workshop to provide support to the group. To this day I wish I had taken pictures of their work in action. The blackboard was divided into four sections that represented four parts of one lab. The teachers were actively engaged in investigating which variables worked best under specific circumstances in order to ensure that the labs they were creating would work every time. Needless to say, the unit the teachers developed was a great success because they had the time to work together to make it highly coherent and to choose activities that would engage all students in concrete experiences and various levels of abstraction.

The teachers used knowledge from research about lesson design, which helped them focus on designing developmentally appropriate activities tied to the learning objectives. For example, science learning cycles (Gillis and MacDougall 2007) and Ruby Payne's work on students of poverty emphasize engaging students with hands-on experiences that move the child "from the specific and concrete to the abstract and general" (Payne 2003, p. 3). The unit was composed of four investigations

that started with concrete ideas and moved to more abstract knowledge. Students first extracted DNA from household objects such as green peppers, onions, and potatoes. The second investigation was designed to show that an enzyme (amylase) can be used to "cut" starch molecules into sugar. The third investigation simulated polymerase chain reactions, and the fourth investigation used an electrophoresis unit to separate components of ink and identify the original sources. This process is an inexpensive substitute for DNA fingerprinting that students can experience in their biology classroom. Not only was the unit that the teachers developed successfully implemented in biology labs, but an article was published in *Education Week* (Hoff 2002) that highlighted the unit. This level of collaboration and the quality of the product produced would not have been possible without the PLC. Through this structure, teachers had the time to examine practice, identify shared goals, and establish a plan for using the new learning materials tied to the district standards and curriculum.

Chemistry Teachers' Revision of Curriculum

Early in the chemistry teachers' collaborative meetings, the chemistry lead teacher informed me that, although the chemistry curriculum had just been written the previous year under the former science coordinator, the chemistry teachers were "unhappy" with the product. After reflecting on the effectiveness of the new curriculum through their PLC work (see Table 7.1, third bullet under Curriculum), they now saw the curriculum's weaknesses and wanted to modify it to improve instruction.

In collaboration with all chemistry teachers and the teacher leader, I reviewed their concerns and agreed with their suggestions for improvement. I proposed that I talk with the director of instruction and asked the teachers if they would pool their multitude of labs from around the district, identify highly effective labs within each unit, and write lessons for labs to be included as an appendix in the curriculum. Our proposal for revisions and the creation of aligned lab activities was accepted by the director of instruction, and several chemistry teachers met for one week during the summer to create a revised chemistry curriculum, complete with lab activities.

These two examples highlight the commitment of the biology and chemistry teachers to collaborate with teacher leaders to examine what is working and enhance the instructional materials for all students throughout the district. They were focused on enhancing student learning and proposed the development and revision of instructional materials that would better enable teachers to meet all students' learning needs. This focus on improving practice and student learning illustrates the quality of these teachers' engagement in their professional learning communities.

Increased Interest in PLCs

As the biology and chemistry PLCs began to flourish, it was not long (the next year) until other teachers expressed interest in the idea of working in a PLC to improve instruction. By the end of the second year of this process, new learning communities formed for teachers of Earth science, Advanced Placement (AP) biology, AP chemistry, oceanography, and physics/AP physics. With a working framework in place for identifying and supporting teacher leaders, and a framework around which PLCs would work, these new teacher collaborative teams quickly began the work of improving student achievement across the district.

Summary of District Support of Teacher Leaders

Teacher leaders, with continuing support from science leadership, have clearly played a critical role in supporting and facilitating content-based PLCs throughout the district. There are two important factors in summarizing the district support of teacher leaders. First, the intention was not to create a new program called a professional learning community. The focus centered on searching for ways for teachers to work together more effectively and efficiently for the purpose of increasing student achievement. Teacher leaders were an essential component of this work. Second, this approach was not "business as usual" in our district. The changes started slowly and grew as the community of teachers became more and more interested in developing additional content-based PLCs.

In addition to creating content-based PLCs among teachers, a community of teacher leaders was also developed among the science department chairs and the teacher leaders. Before this time, the science department chairs would meet once a month to discuss administrative issues. As this community of science department chairs and teacher leaders grew and matured, the discussions centered on what was working and not working with curriculum, assessment, and instruction in terms of increased student achievement.

As illustrated in the examples, school district leaders can support teachers in PLCs that focus on making fundamental changes in teaching and learning. Science leadership must take an active role in identifying dynamic teacher leaders and provide them with professional development and continuing support to enhance their knowledge, skills, and abilities to work with other teachers. In this process, it is important that the science leadership build a shared vision around a framework with the teacher community that provides protocols and guidelines. Ultimately, the science leadership must ensure that the community remains focused on results, with the end result being increased student achievement.

PLCs at the district and school level can also be supported by state-level leadership that is committed to building capacity to support PLCs, as discussed in the next section.

Chapter 7

State Support of Teacher Leaders

The South Carolina Mathematics and Science Unit (MSU), under the leadership of John Holton at the South Carolina Department of Education (SCDOE), is composed of eight regional directors and generally one mathematics specialist and one science specialist within each region, depending on the needs of the region. Since 1993, the MSU has had a rich history of providing professional development and supporting schools and school systems. This program was supported initially by a Statewide Systemic Initiative grant from the National Science Foundation and is now supported by state funds.

In 2003 the MSU began the Mathematics and Science Coaching Initiative (MSCI). In the MSCI model, which originally focused on elementary schools that included kindergarten through fifth grade, there would be one coach for one school and for one subject (either mathematics or science). The MSCI now supports coaches in schools from kindergarten through eighth grade. Middle school coaches are called instructional coaches (iCoaches). Whereas K–5 coaches coach one subject at one school, middle school iCoaches may coach multiple subjects within one school.

The MSCI has two major purposes: (1) to prepare and support school leaders (coaches) to engage teachers in reflective practices and assist them in implementing effective instructional strategies in mathematics and science and (2) to support school learning communities as they plan, implement, and reflect on mathematics and science instruction.

Identifying Coaches

The application process for involvement in the MSCI is rigorous. The application packet includes sections on school demographics, the principal's plan for using coaches in support of the existing school plan, and the coach applicant's vision of his or her role in the context of the school plan. The applications are reviewed and scored by a selected team of respected statewide math/science education professionals from schools, universities, and business/industry. The selection process is supervised by John Holton, and coaches are selected based on application ratings and additional variables such as school ratings, district needs and resources, and equity across the school districts and regions in the state. Schools receive $31,200 from the MSU in support of each coach's salary, and they may use additional state and district funds to support the coach's salary.

The MSCI is designed to be a three- to six-year program. Three themes shape the program: (1) the heart of the work is to improve instruction in mathematics and science, (2) coaching is the chosen path toward improving instruction, and (3) a theoretical framework designed to improve instruction in mathematics and science guides the work of the coach.

National Science Teachers Association

Theoretical Framework to Improve Instruction

The theoretical framework that guides the work of the coach, and thus the professional development provided, is based on the *theory of action* from the Leadership and Assistance for Science Education Reform (LASER) Center of the National Science Resources Center (NSRC 2003). Figure 7.1 is the Theory of Action for Instructional Improvement (TOAII) for the MSU.

The foundation of this model is the support that the MSU provides to the communities. Research, best practices, and analysis of data inform the MSU vision. The vision, in turn, provides guidance on the components of effective improvement infrastructure—competent teachers, research-based curriculum, assessment, instructional materials support, and engaged schools and communities. This all leads to improved classroom instruction and, ultimately, improved student achievement. The bottom half of the TOAII figure reflects the work of the MSU, while the top half reflects the work done in schools. In the background of the top and bottom half are pyramids that represent coaching as the vehicle by which positive change will occur.

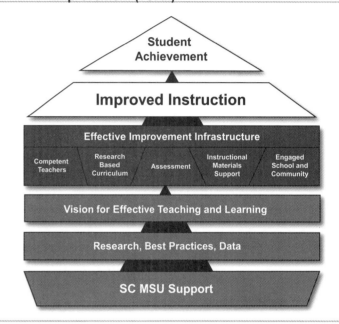

Figure 7.1. South Carolina Mathematics and Science Unit (SC MSU) Theory of Action for Instructional Improvement (TOAII)

Training and Support of Coaches and Administrators

The coaches and their principals and district representatives attend a week of professional development, called the Math/Science Coaching Institute 1 (MSCI1). This week introduces coaches and administrators to the TOAII; explores systems thinking as it applies to making change in a school setting; establishes a community of coaches, administrators, and MSU staff; and assists in the development of a school plan that involves the role of the coach. Coaches attend a second week of the institute (MSCI2) and participate in sessions that enhance their coaching skills and provide them with opportunities to deepen their knowledge of curriculum, standards, and content appropriate to their role in improving instruction.

During the first school year, the coaches also attend monthly learning community meetings (LCMs) that continue to immerse them in understanding the TOAII, coaching, and content standards. During the summer after the first school year in the program, coaches learn best practices in assessment. This theme continues

Chapter 7

throughout the LCMs for the second year. The LCMs occur four times during the second year of the coaching initiative, approximately every other month.

During the summer after the second school year in the program, coaches refine their coaching skills to support PLCs that engage their school community in sustainable instructional improvement efforts. This theme continues throughout the four bimonthly LCMs in the third year.

With the TOAII and coaching as the chosen path to improve instruction, the vision for the MSCI was clear. The MSU staff was composed of about 30 people, including area coordinators and math and science specialists, all with various areas of expertise, so this clarity of vision was a critical factor in bringing the MSU community together to design the initial and continuing professional development and to provide support for the coaches and their administrators. With some hearty discussions, the program for years 1 and 2 were set.

In year 3, it was clear that the framework of PLCs was a powerful model for sustained school improvement. It was also clear that coaching could be an important part of a PLC. However, there were two issues that lacked clarity. One was how the concept of a PLC fit into the TOAII. The second question centered on the vision that the MSU had for PLCs and therefore what the specific professional development and support would look like. The inquiry into answering these questions yielded a slight modification of the TOAII and the creation of a successful year 3 program.

In the NSRC's theory of action, the fifth infrastructure is called School and Community Support and involves creating partnerships with community scientists, organizations, and businesses. The MSU modified this part of the infrastructure to be called engaged school and community and redefined it to reflect the components of creating and maintaining a PLC within the coaching initiative. This step of adapting and creating ownership in a vision and framework is often critical as schools and organizations adopt visions and frameworks that originate from other organizations. Indeed, dialogue and discussions around the fine points of each and every component of the TOAII are what gave the MSU its clarity of vision and community ownership in the process.

The year 3 team was initially composed of 10 MSU staff. In planning the third year of the coaching initiative, it was quickly discovered that there were multiple visions of the purpose, structure, and value of PLCs. With these multiple visions came multiple ideas about what the program would look like. The MSU needed to have a common vision of how the work of a coach could contribute to moving a school toward being a high-functioning PLC focused on student achievement. In this inquiry, there were three critical steps in designing the program.

First, the common vision of the components of a PLC came from an article from the Southwest Educational Development Lab (SEDL) by Leo and Cowan (2000). This article provides succinct insight into the work of Shirley Hord (1997). The year

3 team agreed that this article gave clarity to the components of a PLC. However, the article stressed the importance of the principal. What was the role of the coach? One of the team members drafted an outline of the article and then rephrased the components that were specific to the role of the principal into components that were more appropriate for a coach. At a year 3 planning meeting, the rephrased draft was discussed and further modified by the year 3 team. This document helped create the vision and framework for year 3 professional development for coaches and how the coaches would support PLCs. Table 7.2 includes part of the document.

Table 7.2. Coaches' Role in Creating and Maintaining Professional Learning Communities (PLCs)

Shared and supportive leadership	Coaches in PLCs accept a collegial relationship with teachers, share power and decision making, and promote and nurture leadership development among the staff.
Shared mission and vision	Coaches in PLCs help create and maintain a shared mission and vision among teachers and teacher teams that have an unwavering focus on student learning, support norms of behavior, and guide decisions about teaching and learning in the school.
Collective learning and application of learning	Coaches in PLCs work collaboratively with teachers and teacher teams to solve problems and improve learning opportunities. Together, they seek new knowledge and skills as well as ways to apply their new learning to their work.
Supportive conditions	Coaches in PLCs develop collegial relationships among the teachers as they interact productively toward a goal. Collegial relationships include respect, trust, norms of continuous critical inquiry and improvement, and positive, caring relationships among students, teachers, and administrators. Coaches work with administrators to maximize physical conditions for teacher teams to meet, examine, and improve current practices.
Shared personal practice	Coaches in PLCs help teachers formalize a structure for collegial coaching that is a powerful contributor to PLCs. In such formal interactions, teachers may visit other teachers' classrooms and/or meet on a regular basis to provide encouragement and feedback on new instructional practices.

Source: Adapted with permission of SEDL. Leo, T., and D. Cowan. 2000. *Launching professional learning communities: Beginning actions. Issues ...About Change* 8 (1): 1–15. Available from *www.sedl.org/change/issues/issues81/issues-8.1.pdf.*

One specific outcome of this inquiry was a framework that provided the coaches with a description of their role and work in comparison to that of the principals. For example, many of the books and articles the coaches would read as part of their professional development would stress the role of the principal, not the role of the teacher leader or coach, and the framework would support them in translating their new learning and skills into their roles.

Throughout the first and second years of the program, coaches primarily provided coaching for individual teachers and teacher teams. These teacher teams were typically grade-level teams, but also included other school teams that were focused on issues such as discipline and school improvement. In year 3, the MSU formalized the concept of the PLC as a structure to support collaborative work in schools. Becky DuFour, in the video *Let's Talk About PLC* (DuFour et al. 2003), says that she did not come into a school with a new program called a PLC but rather engaged teachers in a process of continual improvement and later named it a PLC. Likewise, the structure of the PLC within the MSCI is not new to the coaches. It is not "another program" but a structure that coaches use to bring the school together as a

Chapter 7

community in a more effective manner to address student achievement. Note that in the district examples provided earlier in this chapter, science leadership did not announce a new program but was in search of a structure that facilitated an effective and efficient environment focused on student learning and achievement.

The second critical step in designing the program for coaches involved establishing clear roles for the coach and principal in creating and maintaining PLCs. Again, most literature that the coaches would read emphasized the role of the principal. The following two paragraphs illustrate the interdependent and separate roles of the coach and principal.

The year 3 coaches engaged in an activity to help them develop a common understanding of *professional teacher team* and *professional learning community*. Coaches were asked to write their individual definitions of the words *professional, traditional, learning, teacher, team,* and *community*. They then created a definition of a *traditional teacher team* through large-group dialogue. This process was repeated for defining *professional teacher team* and *professional learning community*, and they engaged in discussions to compare and contrast each.

Figure 7.2. Framework for the Work of Coaches and Principals in a Professional Learning Community

Traditional Teacher Teams
(TTTs)

With a common vocabulary created by the community, a framework was proposed (Figure 7.2). In this framework, the coach's role is to assist in the development of grade-level and other teams, known as traditional teacher teams, to become high-functioning, self-sustaining professional learning teams (PLTs). It is the role of the principal to support the role of the coach and to unite the school teams in a PLC. Through this framework, the coaches clearly see their role as a vital component of a PLC. As administrators and coaches read literature on PLCs that emphasize the principal's role in creating and maintaining PLCs, the administrators and the coaches clarify their distinct roles in creating and maintaining PLTs.

The third critical step in creating the professional development program for the year 3 coaches involved the nature of the professional development itself. The MSU made an explicit decision not to "teach" coaches about PLCs, but instead to create a structure where coaches learned about PLCs by participating in a PLC themselves, with the support of the MSU staff. In this model, the coaches formed PLTs composed of three to five members. The MSU PLTs formed by the coaches created their own mission and vision for the work they would do over the course of the year. Based on

National Science Teachers Association

the work at their schools, the MSU PLTs focused on issues such as best practices in assessment, research on high-performing high-poverty schools, and high-functioning PLCs. Each team collectively learned new material and coached each other on the application of the new material in their respective schools.

The MSU supported the MSU PLTs whose purpose was to impact teacher instruction. In turn, the coaches' work with teacher teams at their schools was focused on enhancing student achievement (see Figure 7.3). Notice that this model is in alignment with and gives greater clarity to the TOAII in how the work with coaches is designed to result in improved instruction and improved student achievement.

The professional teaching and learning cycle (PTLC) as outlined in Tobia (2007) was useful to both the MSU PLTs and the school PLTs. At the heart of the PTLC is the use of data to create and implement plans, and then to consistently use data to monitor the plan's effectiveness (see Figure 7.4).

Note that the coaches must have access to data. The coach takes the data (e.g., disaggregated quizzes, unit tests, benchmark tests, state end-of-grade tests) and compiles them into a useful format that is accessible to teachers, who then use the data to make decisions about their instruction. Embedded within this cycle is the need for coaches and teachers to have the knowledge and skills that enable them to engage in dialogue about the meaning of the data. Many of the coaches have found through their experiences that providing teachers with data that are useful and meaningful to them in their context as teachers, engaging them in analysis of the data, and then exploring strategies that can be

Figure 7.3. Model for Mathematics and Science Unit (MSU) Work to Impact Student Achievement

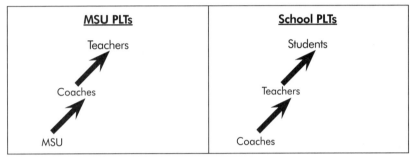

Note: PLTs = professional learning teams.

Figure 7.4. Professional Teaching and Learning Cycle

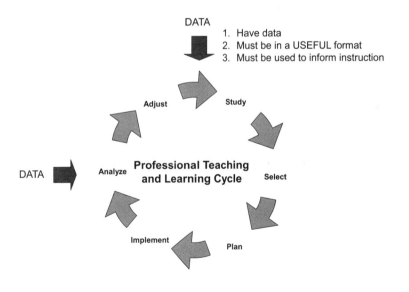

Source: Adapted with permission of SEDL. Tobia, E. 2007. The professional teaching and learning cycle: Implementing a standards-based approach to professional development. *SEDL Letter* 19 (1): 11–15. Available from *www.sedl.org/pubs/sedl-letter/v19n01/SEDLLetter_v19n01.pdf.*

used to address the student learning needs indicated in the data is a more effective approach than giving teachers raw data and telling them what it means and what they should do.

Results From Supporting Coaches

The MSU gathers qualitative and quantitative data to continue to provide effective support and professional development for the coaches as their needs change. They use the data to enhance the professional development program, as well as to document their impact and share with the community at large the changes that are occurring in teachers' classrooms.

The MSU community has hundreds of anecdotal stories that illustrate examples of improved instruction and teacher practice. For example, I witnessed an experienced second-grade classroom teacher change her approach to teaching science from reading textbooks to an inquiring classroom where students are involved in the process of science while learning science. The following story is an example of one of her lessons.

After some discussion about what they were going to do in the lesson, the teacher brought her second-grade students to the oval rug in the corner of the classroom. Students sat together in pairs, and the teacher placed a mealworm on a paper plate in front of each pair of students. She asked them to observe what they saw and to talk with their classmates to compare observations. The students were very excited and were talking about the mealworm, wondering about what it eats, how it eats, and how it drinks. After about five minutes, one student approached the teacher and asked, "May we take out our science notebooks and draw what we see?" Clearly, not only had the teacher changed her approach to teaching science, but the students had changed the ways in which they learned science.

There are many such stories that have not been collected by the MSU, although qualitative data do exist in the coaches' electronic journals. In addition, observational data were collected by Wicker (2006) as part of her dissertation. She compared the instructional practices of science teachers across the state who were coached by MSU coaches with those who were not coached. She found that science teachers who were coached implemented features of inquiry more often and used science kits as the basis of their curriculum more often than did teachers who were not coached.

The following story illustrates the work of the coaches. As part of an assignment, a coach was asked by her MSU specialist to place the science Palmetto Achievement Challenge Test (PACT) scores into an Excel template created by the specialist. The template was designed so that coaches could simply place raw data on student achievement as measured by the state test, and it automatically created graphs to easily analyze patterns over a period of four years. The coach, being energetic, used the template to graph the PACT scores in science, mathematics, social studies, and English language arts (ELA). The MSU specialist and the coach reviewed the graphs, and a pattern immediately emerged (Figure 7.5).

Figure 7.5. School English Language Arts Palmetto Achievement Challenge Test Score Level for Grade 3, 2003–2007

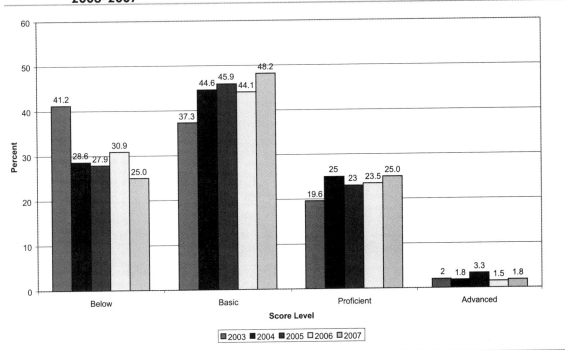

An examination of grade 3 ELA scores over four years revealed that a very low percentage of students achieved at the "advanced" level. Looking at grades 4, 5, 6, 7, and 8, the coach observed that the advanced scores on PACT were all less than 3.3% over a four-year period for all of the grades. Excitement began to build as the specialist declared, "Ninety percent of solving a problem is knowing what the problem is, and I think you did just that!"

With this in mind, the science coach began to formulate a framework around which the entire school could envision schoolwide improvement. The coach was inspired by her MSU experience on writing and reading in the science classroom and the science learning cycle. Additionally, after reading an article by Gillis and MacDougall (2007), the coach saw how the learning cycles could be combined to form one framework for her school (see Table 7.3).

This framework became an integral part of collective learning and application of learning at the school. As teachers learned instructional strategies as part of a schoolwide professional development plan, they explored the application of each

Table 7.3. Framework for Using Instructional Strategies in the Classroom

	Stage 1	Stage 2	Stage 3	Stage 4
Writing cycle	Prepare students to write	Write draft	Edit and revise	Publish
Reading cycle	Prepare students to read	Interactive reading	Student reflection and ownership of material and concepts	Application
Science cycle	Prepare students to learn	Teaching and learning	Student reflection and ownership of material and concepts	Application

strategy and how it could be used in various places in the learning cycles. A graphic organizer, for example, can be used to brainstorm ideas that prepare students for a writing assignment, as a reflection strategy after a reading assignment, or as a reflection strategy after a science lesson.

In addition to the qualitative data discussed so far, the MSU also examines quantitative data to gauge the effectiveness of the program. For example, they analyzed science PACT data to determine the extent to which the coaching initiative was affecting student achievement. Cohort II data were analyzed after completing the third year of the initiative. By the end of the third year, Cohort II was composed of 18 mathematics and 14 science coaches. In this particular inquiry, the MSU Evaluation Committee narrowed the questions to the following:

1. Were there any schools in which PACT scores *increased* from the year prior to entry into the initiative to the third year in the initiative in *all* grades in which PACT was given at that school? (These schools were labeled Group 1.)
2. Where there any schools in which PACT scores *decreased* from the year prior to entry into the initiative to the third year in the initiative in *all* grades in which PACT was given at that school? (These schools were labeled Group 2.)
3. What is the difference between Group 1 and Group 2 schools? What are the common features of schools in Group 1? What are the common features of schools in Group 2?

MSU coordinators and specialists were given a graph of the PACT scores over a four-year period (the year prior to entry into the initiative and the three years of participation in the initiative) for each grade that PACT was administered at each school with which they worked. In addition, each coordinator and specialist was asked to write a brief summary of the school based on the following: the role and effectiveness of the coach, the role and effectiveness of the school and appropriate district administration, the general level of competence of the teachers, the level of use of research-based curriculum, the level of use of best practices in assessment, the organization of instructional materials support, the level of an engaged school and community, and the general school climate.

An analysis of the data revealed that there were factors related to administration and school climate separating the Group 1 schools from the Group 2 schools.

- *Administration:* It was found that the administration in Group 1 schools had a principal who was with the school from the beginning of the program and provided a high degree of support for the role of the coach as guided by the vision framed by the TOAII. Conversely, Group 2 schools had an unstable administration (one school had three principals in three years), included new principals who were not involved at the start of the program and had not attended the professional development with the coach during MSCI1, and perhaps more importantly, generally had a different vision of how to improve student achievement than the vision guided by the TOAII; therefore, these schools were not effective in supporting the coach.
- *School Climate:* Teachers in Group 1 had a systemic approach to using the coach and actively used the coach in planning, observing, and reflecting on lessons. This positive school climate and approach to embedding the role of the coach in the work of the teachers was not apparent at the beginning of the program but evolved over three years of the program. As a result, the coach was actively engaged as a support person for a majority of the teachers at the school. Conversely, Group 2 schools did not develop a systemic approach to taking advantage of the coach, with few teachers actively seeking the support of the coach. Additional data collected by an external evaluator as well as some coaches' personal action research reveal a strong correlation between the number of hours a teacher spent with a coach and student gains on PACT.

In general, the MSU found that fidelity to the program was the key factor in the gains in student achievement over the three years of the initiative.

Summary of State Support of Teacher Leaders

As with the district support of teacher leaders, the MSU initiative began by identifying teachers to serve as leaders and then providing professional development and continuing support that focused on improving student learning and achievement. The intention was not to implement a new program called a professional learning community but to use the strategy of coaching to enhance instruction and then to engage teachers and their coaches in PLCs as a path to improve instruction and student learning and achievement. Additionally, it should be noted that the

Chapter 7

process of change takes time and that increased student achievement may be influenced by the degree to which the school community—administration, coaches, and teachers—have a common vision of improving student learning. A theory of action, initially provided by science leadership and subsequently owned by the community through dialogue and consensus, is a critical factor in providing vision and direction for change.

Conclusion

The 2003 NSTA position statement on leadership in science education (*www. nsta.org/about/positions/leadership.aspx*) emphasizes science leadership roles in creating collaborative work environments and working closely with school and other administrators to improve science instruction, and therefore student achievement. In doing so, science leadership needs to establish and protect time for teachers to work collaboratively and develop clear direction and expectations for the work with teacher leaders and teachers.

In "Science Leadership in an Era of Accountability: A Call for Collaboration," which highlighted the NSTA position statement, it was stated that "major challenges facing science education leadership involve removing barriers that restrict collaboration, while installing systems that facilitate it" (Jorgenson, MacDougall, and Llewellyn 2003, p. 62). It has been shown in this chapter that science leadership is essential for support of teacher leaders and that these teacher leaders are critical advocates for institutional changes that impact curriculum, assessment, instructional practices, and student learning and achievement.

It has been further noted that a theory of action or a framework designed to guide the vision and work of the community provides necessary clarity and direction. This organizational schema needs to be structured in such a way that new information can be assimilated as the program develops. If, however, new information does not fit into the schema, either the information is discarded or the information is accommodated and the schema is revised.

This chapter has examined the role of science leadership in developing and supporting teacher leaders for the purpose of creating and maintaining effective PLCs focused on improving student achievement. In doing so, the science leader must (1) identify teacher leaders who are successful with a variety of students, (2) provide teacher leaders with initial professional development and continuing support that build the skills to bring teachers together as a professional community to improve student learning and achievement, and (3) provide continuing support for the PLC with a clear vision and expectations.

A scientist once said that the expression that spurs the greatest scientific activity is not "Eureka!" but "Huh …?" One could imagine a flurry of questions being created as a result of this simple expression, only to be followed by a series of investigations

126

designed to search for answers. Likewise, it is this expression that also spurs teacher inquiry into identifying best practices that result in improved student achievement in schools. When we return to the question asked at the beginning of the chapter, Are two heads better than one? the hope is that this chapter has provided the evidence that the answer is a resounding YES. Two heads are indeed better than one when supported teacher leaders bring teachers together, bring student data to the table, support teacher dialogue and analysis of the data, and inquire into finding answers to simple questions like "Huh … I wonder why our students …?"

Reflection Questions
- Compare the times when you have worked in a professional team or community with those times you have not. When was it beneficial to work in a team? What variables made the team work well? What were some of the things that prevented teams from being effective?
- What are some of the skills necessary for teacher leaders to bring teachers together to work effectively as a team for the benefit of improving student learning? To what extent are these being supported in your setting?
- Does your school have a shared "framework" for improving student learning? How was it created and who continues to shape it? If not, how might you bring staff together to create such a framework?
- In what ways did this chapter exemplify shared and supportive leadership? What do you hope to see the leaders at your site do to support teacher collaboration focused on science learning?

References
Anderson, G. 2000. Brazosport ISD: Implementation of the quality agenda to ensure excellence and equity for ALL students. Paper presented at the Improving Achievement Outcomes in the Middle Grades Conference sponsored by the Council of Chief State School Officers: Project to Improve Achievement in High Poverty Schools, Long Beach, CA.

DuFour, R., R. Eaker, B. DuFour, and D. Sparks. 2003. *Let's talk about PLC: Getting started.* (Video set.) Bloomington, IN: Solution Tree.

DuFour, R., B. DuFour, R. Eaker, and T. Many. 2006. *Learning by doing: A handbook for professional learning communities at work.* Bloomington, IN: Solution Tree.

Gillis, V. R., and G. MacDougall. 2007. Reading to learn science as an active process. *The Science Teacher* 74 (5): 45–50.

Hoff, D. J. 2002. Biology classes analyzing genetics. *Education Week* 21 (25): 1, 20–21.

Hord, S. 1997. *Professional learning communities: Communities of continuous improvement.* Austin, TX: Southwest Educational Development Laboratory.

Chapter 7

Jorgenson, O., G. MacDougall, and D. Llewellyn. 2003. Science leadership in an era of accountability: A call for collaboration. *Science Educator* 12 (1): 59–64.

Kagan, L., and S. Kagan. 2000. *Cooperative learning course workbook.* San Clemente, CA: Kagan Publishing and Professional Development.

Langford, D. P. 2002. *Quality learning training manual.* Molt, MT: Langford International.

Leo, T., and D. Cowan. 2000. Launching professional learning communities: Beginning actions. *Issues About Change* 8 (1): 1–16.

Lipton, L., and B. Wellman. 1998. *Pathways to understanding: Patterns and practices in the learning-focused classroom.* 3rd ed. Sherman, CT: MiraVia.

National Science Resources Center (NSRC). 2003. *The LASER Center: Leadership and Assistance for Science Education Reform.* http://www.nsrconline.org/pdf/laser.pdf

Payne, R. 2003. *Understanding and working with students and adults from poverty: Building learning structures inside the head.* Highlands, TX: aha! Process.

Tobia, E. 2007. The professional teaching and learning cycle: Implementing a standards-based approach to professional development. *SEDL Letter* 19 (1): 11–15.

Usdan, M., B. McCloud, and M. Podmostko. 2001. *Leadership for student learning: Redefining the teacher as leader.* Washington, DC: Institute for Educational Leadership.

Wicker, R. K. 2006. Do science coaches promote inquiry-based instruction in the elementary science classroom? Ph.D. diss., Clemson University.

Chapter 8

K20 Model:
Creating Networks, Professional Learning
Communities, and Communities of Practice
That Increase Science Learning

Linda Atkinson, Jean M. Cate, Mary John O'Hair, and Janis Slater

"We live in a world of possibilities…
when we believe it, we'll see it."

—Dewitt Jones (2007)

Chapter 8

For over a decade, the K20 Center at the University of Oklahoma has promoted systemic "whole-school" reform through a school-university network in urban, suburban, and small-town settings, although the majority are rural schools. This systemic model develops professional learning communities (PLCs) and has been successful in district-wide and school initiatives across Oklahoma. Research findings show that teachers increase efficacy, content knowledge, and use of inquiry, and students increase their interest in science and improve learning as measured by classroom and state assessments (McKean and Fredman 2008).

The K20 Model is designed to transform conventional schools into PLCs by using shared leadership development, regional networking, and two guiding systemic frameworks—IDEALS and 10 Practices of High-Achieving Schools (O'Hair, McLaughlin, and Reitzug 2000)—to establish conditions in schools that promote continuous learning. IDEALS is an acronym for Inquiry, Discourse, Equity, Authenticity, Leadership, and Service (see Table 8.1). This serves as a guiding framework for the K20 Center model and is supported by the evidence-based 10 Practices (see Table 8.2). Together they provide interactive and mutually dependent processes and practices to help transform teaching, learning, and leading in ways that meet the challenges of today's rapidly changing world.

Table 8.1. IDEALS Framework

The K20 Center's IDEALS framework sets the stage for the 10 research-based practices linked directly to high student achievement. IDEALS is an acronym for Inquiry, Discourse, Equity, Authenticity, Leadership, and Service.

Inquiry is the critical study of our practice by gathering and considering data, new knowledge, and other's perspectives. The primary purpose of inquiry is the improvement of our individual practice and our school's practice.

Discourse refers to conversations, discussions, and debates focused on teaching and learning issues. Discourse nurtures professional growth, builds relationships, results in more informed practice, and improves student achievement.

Equity refers to seeking fair and just practices both within and outside the school.

Authenticity (authentic achievement) refers to learning that is genuine and connected rather than something that is fake and fragmented. Teachers who practice authenticity help students connect learning to life.

Leadership (shared leadership) in schools is the development of shared understandings that lead to a common focus and improve the school experience for all members of the school community.

Service refers to the belief that making a difference in the lives of children and families requires serving the needs of the community as well as the school.

Source: Adapted from O'Hair, M. J., H. J. McLaughlin, and U. C. Reitzug. 2000. *The foundation of democratic education.* Fort Worth, TX: Harcourt Brace.

Table 8.2. Ten Practices of High-Achieving Schools

To improve student achievement, schools develop, implement, and sustain the "10 Practices of High-Achieving Schools" (O'Hair, McLaughlin, and Reitzug 2000).

Practice 1: Shared Vision

A shared set of goals, commitments, and practices enacted throughout the school. The shared school vision serves as a basis for decision making and change (i.e., "How does that decision fit with what we believe in?") and gives individuals an enhanced sense of purpose. They make individuals part of a bigger cause, a cause beyond one's self (O'Hair, McLaughlin, and Reitzug 2000). Sergiovanni (2001) emphasizes that "the vision of a school must reflect the hopes and dreams, the needs and interests, the values and beliefs of everyone who has a stake in the school: teachers, parents, and students" (p. 149).

Practice 2: Authenticity

Students' learning experiences are optimized when instruction is authentic and challenging, demands skills, and allows for student autonomy (Yair 2000). When schools demonstrate high expectations and have a common intellectual mission, student performance is enhanced and gaps are decreased (Newmann 2007).

Practice 3: Shared Leadership

Hargreaves and Fink (2006) contend that professional learning communities (PLCs) "embody the most positive features of distributed leadership, bringing the energy and ability of the whole community forward to serve the best interest of all students" (p.128). Building leadership capacity and structures to support shared governance represents innovative, visionary elements of the school improvement process in creating and sustaining PLCs.

Practice 4: Personalized Environments

Over the past few decades, large schools have become a way of life across the United States and the number continues to increase. Wasley (2002) suggests that these large schools lessen the educational quality for disadvantaged students and indicates that small schools and small classes increase the success for students.

Practice 5: Teacher Collaboration

Collaboration has been called the single most important factor in sustaining the effort to create a PLC (DuFour and Eaker 1998); and there is evidence of improved student learning in schools with collaborative norms (Lee and Smith 1996; Louis, Kruse, and Marks 1996; Newmann and Wehlage 1995; Schmoker 1999).

Practice 6: Inquiry and Discourse

PLCs use data-driven decision-making strategies, set SMART (specific, measurable, attainable, realistic, and time-bound) goals, and incorporate data analysis to promote collaborative dialogue (Schmoker 2006). Bernhardt (2000) identified four types of data (demographic, perceptual, student learning, and school process data) that can help educators monitor and assess improvement progress.

Practice 7: Supportive Leaders

Research by Marzano, Waters, and McNulty (2005) emphasizes the importance of the principal as a leader of educational reform, understanding the changes that impact student learning and what these changes require of the teachers. Principal leadership continues to be identified as the key factor in the success of PLCs (DuFour and Eaker 1998; Huffman and Hipp 2003; Sergiovanni 2001), yet the principal's role has changed dramatically.

Practice 8: Community Connections

Schools and teachers should attempt to create more family-like schools (Epstein and Salinas 2004), viewing families and communities as partners in the educational process and having common and shared interests and goals for their students' success. The obligation of schools goes beyond just school-home communication, extending to connecting and collaborating with families and communities throughout the educational process.

Practice 9: Equity Concerns

A concern for equity results in asking and acting on questions such as What makes this a best practice? Does it work for all students, or for only some students? Does it serve to keep students under control, or does it enhance intellectual growth? Is there a difference? (O'Hair, McLaughlin, and Reitzug 2000). Effective schools are culturally responsive to racial, ethnic, and culture groups, incorporating these as a framework for understanding and inquiry (Banks et al. 2007).

Practice 10: External Expertise

Research shows that networks, partnerships, and coalitions provide schools with strong support for successful transformation to PLCs (Lieberman and Miller 2007).

Chapter 8

The K20 Center helps schools develop learning teams to address the 10 Practices in their schools. The process encompasses five phases: Phase I is the development of shared leadership; Phase II is whole-school learning, especially around technology integration; Phase III is STEM (science, technology, engineering, and mathematics) teacher development; Phase IV is student engagement; and Phase V is engaged scholarship.

The K20 Center model forms nested professional development communities, starting with statewide and regional networks that prepare school-based leaders to develop PLCs in their local sites. Within all of these PLCs, leaders and teachers work together to create communities of practice that focus on making changes in teacher classroom practice to produce classrooms that are communities for inquiry. The work is aimed at increasing student learning in science.

Theory Into Practice

The K20 Model is based on four interrelated structures for engaging people in communities: networks, PLCs, communities of practice, and classroom communities for inquiry. The K20 program drew on the theory and research on each of these types of communities to inform the program model. Discussions of key research findings and theory from each area illustrate why and how the K20 Model uses these ideas in its design. Applications in practice related to theory are described.

Networks
Theory and Research
Scholars from multiple disciplines have called for a greater clarification of network theory; however, today it remains in its infancy. Emerging themes from a multitude of network studies highlight the following traditions for networks:

- *Positional networking* or focusing on position or roles (Weber 1947), which consists of job-alike networking with principals meeting together or science teachers sharing experiences with other science teachers;
- *Relational networking* or focusing primarily on the direct communication among network participants that reduces isolation and establishes trust (O'Hair and Veugelers 2005);
- *Cultural networking* or seeking to understand symbols, meanings, and customs within and across organizations (Schein 2004); and
- The new emerging *technological networking* or "networked societies," characterized by interacting with diverse others across multiple networks and flattened hierarchies (Friedman 2005; Haythornthwaite and Wellman 2002).

Educational networks encompass these four traditions and emerge from our knowledge of communal structures and their impact on learning. Much evidence exists that schools successful in transforming themselves have access to external sources of support or networks (Allen and Hensley 2005; Darling-Hammond and McLaughlin 1995; Lieberman and Miller 1990, 2007; Newmann and Wehlage 1995). In reality, networks are professional communities on a larger scale (Lieberman and Miller 2007) helping to shape new forms of professional development that better represent what we know about adult learning and sustaining change over time. These networks increase professional interaction and learning across, and ultimately within, schools and, for those who participate in them, they generate excitement about teaching and learning (Hargreaves and Goodson 2005). School-university networks are becoming an important method to enhance education renewal and student achievement from prekindergarten through graduate education (O'Hair and Veugelers 2005). Historically, these networks have combined positional, relational, and cultural traditions, and educators are beginning to witness the profound impact that the new technological tradition is having on networking theory, research, and practice.

Practice

The K20 school-university network supports continuous learning of multiple stakeholders, beginning with school and district leaders (over 1,200 to date). K20 works with leaders to help them understand and implement strategies that effective leaders use to impact student learning, including establishment and stewardship of a shared vision, building the capacity of the members of a school community, and providing supportive conditions for collaboration and positive learning cultures (Leithwood et al. 2004).

Most K20 network schools begin a renewal process when their principal and/or superintendent enter the network and participate in leadership professional development. The yearlong K20 professional development supports leaders as they learn to create supportive conditions for implementing and sustaining PLCs using the IDEALS and the 10 Practices. The K20 Center uses technology as a catalyst for the development of collaborative structures for school change (Atkinson et al. 2008; Burns 2002).

K20 connects leaders who participate in its science and technology initiatives through networking and continuous learning. Using the Concerns-Based Adoption Model (CBAM; Hall and Hord 2006) as a planning tool, leaders begin to identify and plan strategies for addressing teacher concerns about using new practices, while increasing their skill level and confidence for implementing technology. For example, leaders model technology use by creating multimedia presentations for faculty meetings, adding collaborative processes, implementing online communication mechanisms, and bringing teams of teachers to an annual conference hosted by the

K20 Center to provide them with information and share best practices for school improvement and technology integration. Leaders write an action plan for establishing a shared vision, which is Practice 1 for high-achieving schools (see Table 8.2). Leaders develop leadership teams within their schools, and together they translate the schools' visions across each unique school culture and work collaboratively with teachers to deepen their learning. As a result, the K20 network expands to help leaders as they work within their own schools to develop broad-based PLCs.

PLCs

Theory and Research

Hierarchical governance structures of traditional schools are characterized by a division of labor whereby teachers are in control of the technical core of teaching, such as what is taught and how it is taught, and how to group and grade students, while school leaders serve as a buffer from outside agencies. Schools that are more democratic create interdependency among school leaders, teachers, and community members, providing structures that facilitate participation and communication, fostering cooperation across the community (Furman and Shields 2003). In a PLC, shared vision is developed democratically by school and community members (Eaker, DuFour, and DuFour 2002; O'Hair, McLaughlin, and Reitzug 2000).

The ability to convert vision into action is apparent in successful schools and forms the basis of successful PLCs (Sergiovanni 2005). Schools that involve staff members in focused collaborative sharing and learning based on a shared purpose are described as PLCs (Hord 1997; Wells and Feun 2007). PLCs build the leadership capacity of all stakeholders (Lambert 2003) while distributing leadership across the community (Spillane, Halverson, and Diamond 1999).

Technology can serve as a catalyst for PLC development, giving leaders and teachers a focus for shared learning and leadership. When teachers begin to work together to integrate technology, collective learning is enhanced and a sense of community emerges (Burns 2002; Dexter, Seashore, and Anderson 2002; Riel and Fulton 2001; Williams et al. 2008). As teachers work together toward authenticity and technology integration, they collectively gain knowledge, share best practices, and work collaboratively to build leadership capacity. Technology expands access to a larger community of learners and allows leaders and teachers to exchange ideas with each other and with experts in their content areas. Using technology, teachers can visit classrooms of exemplary instructors; interact with instructors from differing levels (e.g., middle and high school, undergraduate, graduate); receive coaching from their mentors via internet conferencing; and access online portals and virtual libraries (Loucks-Horsley et al. 2003). Working in a collaborative learning environment that involves technology implementation, teachers are more likely to change their own teaching practice to actively involve students (Riel and Fulton 2001).

Empirical evidence suggests that student achievement is significantly higher in schools that function as PLCs than in conventional schools, and those gains also are distributed more equitably (Atkinson et al. 2008; Williams et al. 2008). PLCs can also reduce remoteness and isolation affecting rural teachers' learning (Malhoit and Gottoni 2003).

Practice

The K20 Center supports schools through the change process to become a PLC. In our model, technology integration is pivotal in the change and learning process. Schools focus on implementing 3 of the 10 Practices through the IDEALS. K20 professional development specialists assist school leaders and representative learning teams in implementing the learning goals of the school and facilitate professional development that focuses on the selected three practices and on integration of technology. The yearlong professional development includes time for the entire faculty to meet and learn, time for learning teams to collaborate and plan, opportunities for small groups of teachers to learn together, and just-in-time assistance. Professional development specialists work with the administrator(s) and teachers on each school's learning team to create individualized support plans based on the school's needs and goals. The learning team provides the leadership core for each school that gives the PLC ownership of the professional development and provides a mechanism for building and sustaining capacity within each school for authentic integration of technology using best practices.

The individualized professional development component meets the specific needs of each school for implementation of their grant goals and the specific technology they purchase. At an initial grant-planning meeting, the K20 staff and the school administrator and learning team collaboratively generate a plan for the yearlong professional development process. Over the course of the year, teachers receive over 30 hours of professional development in regular monthly sessions. These sessions are supplemented by quarterly meetings, site visits, a winter conference, and continued communication and collaboration with teachers via e-mail, teleconferences, or phone conversations.

Within the sessions, the K20 specialists act as teachers, modeling various processes and the use of technology, and the teachers are the students. Every session begins with a discussion in which teachers share the experiences they are having with the new approaches in the interval between the professional development sessions. This sharing is followed by an activity in which teachers work in collaborative groups on authentic or problem-based activities. The activities are relevant to teachers, building on their prior knowledge of a situation and offering opportunities for collaboration and personal reflection. These experiences and the time for reflection enable the teachers to use and adapt the authentic experiences and technology-integration strategies that are modeled in the activities.

Chapter 8

Communities of Practice
Theory and Research

When members of a school community come together through democratic processes and form small interest groups, they often develop into communities of practice that facilitate learning of both explicit and tacit knowledge across a community (Wenger 1998). Multiple communities of practice compose effective PLCs (Cate, Vaughn, and O'Hair 2006). Communities of practice develop when teachers who meet regularly develop a sense of trust and purpose, share knowledge, and create products (Printy 2008). Working through difficulties and struggles associated with teaching and learning can be one of the most powerful learning experiences for a working group of teachers (Lieberman and Miller 2007). A strong sense of community enhances information flow, learning support, group commitment, collaboration, and learning satisfaction and results in increased student achievement (Huffman and Hipp 2003; Williams et al. 2008).

Communities of practice provide opportunities for teachers to ask questions, share best practices, and support each other through the struggle of implementing new practices. They may consist of grade-level teachers all implementing the same new curriculum materials or be more schoolwide, in the case of schools working to enhance inquiry in all science classrooms. When principals and teachers operate in an environment of trust, communities of practice are strengthened (Printy and Marks 2006). Teachers also learn from being members of more than one community of practice and from immersion in other levels of community involvement, which in turn supports the overall development of the PLC.

Practice

The K20 Center establishes communities of practice through adapted lesson study focused on inquiry instruction, horizontal and vertical planning, and reading integration. Science specialists use a framework centered on the essentials of inquiry as described in the *National Science Education Standards* (NRC 1996), along with the learning research synthesized by Bransford, Brown, and Cocking (1999), to inform the design and implementation of science professional development. Inquiry learning is modeled in professional development sessions, and teachers are encouraged and supported in implementing new strategies such as inquiry instruction, authentic teaching, and cross-curricular lessons. Using an adapted lesson study approach, teachers collaboratively implement and examine new instructional practices through observation and reflection. As teachers begin to make substantive changes in their teaching, facilitated by professional development embedded within the community of practice, process and content are integrated to produce essential student learning. As teacher practice evolves and changes, student collaboration increases through the use of the discovery process, and classroom communities for inquiry emerge.

Classroom Communities for Inquiry
Theory and Research

Leading educators have called for changes in classroom instruction and interactions to improve the quality of educational experiences. Sergiovanni (1994) proposed that classrooms become communities of learning, caring, and inquiring. Others point to the need for more authentic assignments that engage students in (1) constructing knowledge by organizing, interpreting, evaluating, or synthesizing data; (2) disciplined inquiry and elaborated communication; and (3) extending learning through value beyond the classroom (Newmann and Wehlage 1995). Instructional strategies that engage students provide experiential learning, meaningfulness, and reflection and facilitate the development of knowledge that can be applied to a variety of contexts and problems (Bransford, Brown, and Cocking 1999). Student engagement that produces authentic intellectual work improves student scores on standardized tests (Newmann, Bryk, and Nagoka 2001) and increases student motivation to learn (Greene et al. 2004; Roeser, Midgley, and Urdan 1996).

Authentic intellectual work is associated with higher levels of student achievement (Lee and Smith 1996), which benefits *all* students, regardless of school level, size, context, ethnicity, or socioeconomic status (Smith, Lee, and Newmann 2001). The effectiveness of authentic student engagement is supported by substantiated theory on how students learn (Bransford, Brown, and Cocking 1999; Good and Brophy 1999; Hannafin and Land 1997; Jonassen 1999). The essentials of inquiry as stated in the *National Science Education Standards* focus on scientifically oriented questions, giving priority to responding to evidence in answering questions, formulating explanations from evidence, connecting explanations to existing knowledge, and communicating and justifying explanations. Inquiry learning is the quintessential example of authentic learning because it allows students to construct relevant knowledge in much the same way that practicing scientists examine the natural world. It fosters the integration of content and process while supporting the development of meaningful knowledge representation and concept understanding.

Practice

The K20 Model provides support for teachers to embed inquiry into their classroom practice by creating environments that are learner centered, knowledge centered, assessment centered, and community centered (Bransford, Brown, and Cocking 1999). K20 science specialists share research-based principles on how students learn and help teachers identify strategies for inquiry-based teaching, materials management, classroom management, and assessing student learning. Changes in teacher practice are facilitated through sustained professional development based on individual school goals and needs and continuing support for

integrating authentic instruction using inquiry methodology. Teachers are placed in the role of learners as inquiry is modeled for them in professional development sessions targeting learning pedagogy and specific authentic content. Using adapted lesson study, K20 specialists help teachers frame science instruction around student engagement in the learning process rather than by teacher behavior. Teachers collaborate to identify practices that result in increased student engagement and higher-order intellectual processing. This collaboration allows the classroom culture to shift from teacher centered to student centered and draws on a framework of student learning that emphasizes conceptual understanding, prior knowledge, and social interaction (Bransford, Brown, and Cocking 1999).

K20 Model's Nested Communities

The K20 science model develops nested communities consisting of networks, PLCs, communities of practice, and classroom communities of inquiry that foster connections across levels of collaboration. Teacher practice is enhanced through learning and leadership across concentric communities to improve science education. Within this supportive environment, classroom communities of inquiry are able to move toward more authentic instructional practice through the use of inquiry pedagogy and related student-centered approaches to science learning (see Figure 8.1).

The following sections provide two examples of how the K20 model is working within schools.

Figure 8.1. K20 science concentric communities are nested and focused on producing classrooms of inquiry.

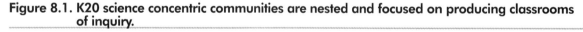

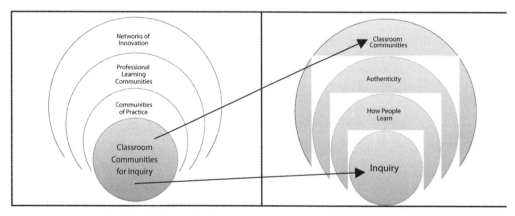

Statewide Initiative With Individual Schools

The K20 Center model is being implemented through the statewide science professional development institute (PDI) sponsored by the Oklahoma Commission for Teacher Preparation. In this project, K20 staff who are former K–8 science teachers and administrators work with teachers and leaders from schools that have received a science PDI grant to use quality science materials and technology and participate in professional development. The goals of the project are to (1) deepen content and pedagogical knowledge of K–8 science teachers through authentic experiences, (2) transfer and sustain teachers' use of authentic instruction in order to advance teaching for conceptual understanding, and (3) create professional communities of practice that provide meaningful experiences within a PLC. The K20 Science PDI engages science teachers in a yearlong process during which each teacher and the school's science learning team (teachers and administrators) are involved in approximately 10 days of professional development with stipends or release time. During year 2 of participation, participants receive follow-up support focused on sustaining inquiry practices, and any new teachers receive professional development. School leaders participate in the K20 leadership seminar with other administrators from across the state to assist them in implementing strategies for developing shared vision, shared leadership, and supportive conditions for authentic teaching. They also attend science-specific leadership sessions to help them implement and support the National Science Teachers Association's essential elements of science reform.

> ## NSTA Position Statement
> Essential elements of science education reform include
> - aligning curriculum, instruction, and assessment with national, state, and local standards;
> - implementing professional development based on district and state needs and objectives; and
> - ensuring that the infrastructure needed to sustain the science program over time is firmly in place.
>
> Source: *www.nsta.org/about/positions/leasdership.aspx*

Elementary and middle schools receive research-based science kits appropriate to each grade level, mostly from Full Option Science System (FOSS), and technology for the school that supports authentic instruction. Professional development is

planned around individual school data and needs and includes how children learn, qualities of effective science instruction, authenticity (inquiry) pedagogy, science kit use, technology integration, classroom management, and collaborative lesson planning. K20 specialists provide onsite support through development of communities of practice within and across grade levels using adaptive lesson integration, technical assistance, coaching, and mentoring.

Communities of practice have developed over the last three years of the science PDI through sustained time for teachers to work on inquiry science implementation and integration. Leaders report that students are doing more hands-on activities and are more actively engaged because teachers are using more inquiry and technology in their science teaching (McKean and Fredman 2008). After participating in the PDI, a number of schools have either adopted inquiry-based science instructional materials in lieu of textbooks or plan to do so in the next science adoption cycle. A participating school district in eastern Oklahoma has a number of schools that have worked closely with the K20 Center, including two science PDI schools. The district has centered its internal and external professional development on PLCs and has attributed recent increases in the district's state accountability score to this collaborative form of teacher learning (Spaulding 2008). A science PDI principal from the district commented, "Since moving to professional learning communities, this faculty has become more collaborative....We always talked about instruction [before the grant]; however, we never honored collaboration by providing a specific time for it. We do that now."

Results have shown an increase in teachers' science learning, confidence, and inquiry usage as well as a significant impact on student learning. On the 2007–2008 teachers' pre/post survey, significant changes over time occurred for nine items—two of which related to teachers' understanding of science teaching and seven of which related to teachers' confidence in teaching science (McKean and Fredman 2008). Reflecting on a recent science lesson in which students predict and investigate what happens when two substances are combined, a fourth-grade teacher remarked that the students were more independent and more willing to come up with their own answers.

Science kit module assessment results showed that first- through eighth-grade students exhibited statistically significant growth in knowledge in the various science topics covered in the modules. After the K20 science PDI, the percentage of students who were proficient on the science state assessment increased by 50%. The greatest shift was evident in a reduction of the proportion of students who scored in the third quartile and a concomitant increase in the proportion scoring in the first quartile.

District-wide Science and Technology Initiative

Another example of the K20 model in action is the District-wide Technology Project (DSTP). Its purpose is to improve the understanding of science content and to implement inquiry-based strategies in science classrooms. Science kits were selected that are research based and aligned with Oklahoma Priority Academic Student Skills and the National Science Education Standards. Through the K20 partnership, teachers attend professional development sessions focused on standards-based curriculum, authentic inquiry lesson development, and research-based teaching strategies in science. Teachers also receive interactive whiteboards and coaching for integration of the new technology with science and other subjects.

School leaders support science education by providing time for professional development, arranging extended plan times for teachers to meet and learn, and providing resources. To learn how to better support instructional change, leaders attend leadership professional development, meet with teacher teams, and observe classroom practices (Darling-Hammond et al. 2007). Multiple site-based teams have formed, as has a district leadership cadre. The communities of practice and leadership teams share best practices, learn together, and address issues and challenges.

Annual teacher assessments that measure technology use and beliefs, science communities of practice, teacher efficacy for science teaching, and teacher use of science processes showed significant changes over the three-year project. Pre/post survey data indicated an increase in teacher confidence in teaching science using a variety of inquiry-based strategies and technology integration in content areas. Teachers reported a significant increase in their ability to monitor students while they participate in hands-on activities. Teacher descriptions of inquiry gained in depth and breath, especially in their descriptions of their roles as facilitators of inquiry. Through communities of practice, teachers began asking reflective questions about their students' learning, opened up their practices to share ideas and experiences of inquiry in their classrooms, increased the teaching of science as well as the science integration into other content areas, and gave deeper consideration of their practices. Teachers shared the following comments:

First-grade teacher: Once the students were involved in the science processes, they picked up on the concepts faster than what we expected.

Second-grade teacher: I didn't have to do everything during the lesson. My students became responsible for their own learning.

Third-grade teacher: The students' prior knowledge might not be what we think it is.

Fourth-grade teacher: We often take what students know for granted.

Fifth-grade teacher: Inquiry instills confidence in students because they are encouraged to find answers.

Students were engaged and enthusiastic about their participation in science investigations. A science routine was established in classrooms with science notebooking and integration of science, reading, and mathematics. Student assessments showed increased science learning on unit assessments ($N = 549$, $p \sim 0.000$) (McKean and Fredman 2008). In 2008, the middle school was awarded the U.S. Department of Education Blue Ribbon Schools award, and the principal acknowledged the work of the K20 Center as a contributor to that award.

Lessons Learned

Through the past several years of working within science initiatives and building PLCs and communities of practice, several lessons have been learned. These lessons have informed our practice and have reinforced for us the importance of the IDEALS framework in our work with schools (see Table 8.1). First, leadership is critical. Leadership is spread across the community and may include district administrators, school leaders, and teacher leaders. Ongoing activities and events for leaders are necessary to support them in building productive communities and bringing about classroom changes. When school leaders create supportive conditions for teachers, the implementation of inquiry science and technology is intensified. Supportive conditions include the availability of professional development structures, modeling, engagement, and relationship building. When district administrators foster the development of school leaders, implementation moves more quickly and systemically. Involvement of leaders in K20's shared leadership and technology integration process before implementing inquiry-based science was a positive indicator of the speed of implementation.

The need for establishing adaptive conditions to fit the culture of each school is another lesson learned. Developing teacher leadership enables substantive change through conversations and reflections with K20 specialists and promotes long-term sustainability. Each school is unique, and establishing a collaborative structure differs in each type and size of school. This requires the program to be ready and able to tailor professional development to meet individual school needs within the broader framework of the overall program goals. Professional development should function within the existing community in order to be effective. K20 specialists develop personal relationships with the faculty in their schools, and, as a result, a level of trust is established that allows them to become an integrated part of the community of practice. When ownership of professional learning lies within the community itself and professional development is adapted to the needs of the individuals within the community, changes in teaching practice occur across the school.

Establishing a shared vision that includes not only school direction and goals but also core principles for teaching and learning makes a difference in the extent of implementation of student-centered science instruction. Implementing inquiry science is more than an instructional strategy; it is a pedagogy that promotes learner responsibility and high-quality intellectual work. Schools with core principles that are compatible with this philosophy have greater success in embedding these practices into their existing classroom communities and developing PLCs.

Conclusion

Professional development for science teachers alone will not produce significant improvements in student achievement. "When professional development is thought of as a discrete program, a series of formal scheduled events, or is otherwise disconnected from authentic problem solving, it is unlikely to have much influence on teacher or student learning" (Hawley and Valli 2007, p. 132). This chapter highlights the importance of first establishing a strong and supportive foundation for continuous learning through school leader professional development and a systemic, substantive whole-school change approach involving PLCs and communities of practice. Synergy exists in schools that have supportive conditions and supportive leaders, allowing them to adopt inquiry practices faster than schools that do not make shared leadership and shared learning a priority. The widely shared sense of community fostered in these schools allows science communities of practice to emerge that increase teacher efficacy, teacher content knowledge, use of inquiry, and students' interest in science and learning, resulting in higher scores on classroom and state assessments. This nested community model builds the capacity of educators and connects them in the common goal of enhancing student learning.

Reflection Questions

- How are school principals and district administrators involved in science education? How are they learning about the needs of science education and what inquiry science looks like?
- What supportive conditions facilitate or impede the development of PLCs? What communities of practice exist across your PLCs to enhance learning and sharing for teachers? How do these differ in various contexts?
- What role does technology play in classrooms? What professional development supports the collaborative engagement of teachers to learn new technologies and engage students?
- What is your shared vision for science teaching and learning and how is it communicated, implemented, maintained, and stewarded in your context?

Chapter 8

References

Allen, L., and F. Hensley. 2005. School-university networks that improve student learning: Lessons from the league of professional schools. In *Network learning for educational change*, eds. W. Veugelers and M. J. O'Hair, 17–32. Maidenhead, UK: Open University Press.

Atkinson, L., M. J. O'Hair, H. D. O'Hair, and L. A. Williams. 2008. Developing and sustaining schools as technology-enriched learning organizations. *I-Manager's Journal on School Educational Technology* 3 (4): 17–33.

Banks, J. A., P. Cookson, G. Gay, W. D. Hawley, J. J. Irvine, S. Nieto, J. W. Schofield, and W. G. Stephen. 2007. Essential principles for teaching and learning for a multicultural society. In *The keys to effective schools: Educational reform as continuous improvement,* ed. W. D. Hawley, 173–188. Thousand Oaks, CA: Corwin Press.

Bernhardt, V. L. 2000. Intersections: New routes open when one type of data crosses another. *Journal of Staff Development* 21 (1): 33–36.

Bransford, J. D., A. L. Brown, and R. R. Cocking, eds. 1999. *How people learn: Brain, mind, experience, and school.* Washington, DC: National Academy Press.

Burns, M. 2002. From compliance to commitment: Technology as a catalyst for communities of learning. *Phi Delta Kappan* 84 (4): 295–302.

Cate, J. M., C. A. Vaughn, and M. J. O'Hair. 2006. A 17-year case study of an elementary school's journey: From traditional school to learning community to democratic school community. *Journal of School Leadership* 16: 86–111.

Darling-Hammond, L., and M. W. McLaughlin. 1995. Policies that support professional development in an era of reform. *Phi Delta Kappan* 74 (10): 753–761.

Darling-Hammond, L., M. LaPointe, D. Meyerson, and M. Orr. 2007. *Preparing school leaders for a changing world: Lessons from exemplary leadership development programs.* Stanford, CA: Stanford Educational Leadership Institute, Stanford University and The Wallace Foundation.

Dexter, S., K. R. Seashore, and R. E. Anderson. 2002. Contributions of professional community to exemplary use of ICT. *Journal of Computer Assisted Learning* 18: 489–497.

DuFour, R., and R. Eaker. 1998. *Professional learning communities at work: Best practices for enhancing student achievement.* Bloomington, IN: National Educational Service.

Eaker, R., R. DuFour, and R. DuFour. 2002. *Getting started: Reculturing schools to become professional learning communities.* Bloomington, IN: National Educational Service.

Epstein, J. L., and K. C. Salinas. 2004. Partnering with families and communities. *Educational Leadership* 61 (8): 12–18.

Friedman, T. 2005. *The world is flat: A brief history of the twenty-first century.* New York: Farrar, Straus and Giroux.

Furman, G. C., and C. M. Shields. 2003. How can educational leaders promote and support social justice and democratic community in schools? Paper presented at the annual meeting of the American Educational Research Association, Chicago.

Good, T. L., and J. E. Brophy. 1999. *Looking in classrooms.* 8th ed. New York: Allyn and Bacon.

Greene, B. A., R. B. Miller, H. M. Crowson, B. L. Duke, and C. L. Akey. 2004. Relations among student perceptions of classroom structures, perceived ability, achievement goals, and cognitive engagement and achievement in high school language arts. *Contemporary Educational Psychology* 29 (4): 462–482.

Hall, G. E., and S. M. Hord. 2006. *Implementing change: Patterns, principles, and potholes.* 2nd ed. Boston: Allyn and Bacon.

Hannafin, M. J., and S. M. Land. 1997. The foundations and assumptions of technology-enhanced, student-centered learning environments. *Instructional Science* 25: 167–202.

Hargreaves, A., and D. Fink. 2006. *Sustainable leadership.* San Francisco: Jossey-Bass.

Hargreaves, A., and I. Goodson. 2005. Series editors' preface. In *Network learning for educational change*, eds. W. Veugelers and M. J. O'Hair, 72–97. Maidenhead, UK: Open University Press.

Hawley, W. D., and L. Valli. 2007. Design principles for learner-centered professional development. In *The keys to effective schools: Educational reform as continuous improvement*, ed. W. D. Hawley, 117–137. Thousand Oaks, CA: Corwin Press.

Haythornthwaite, C., and B. Wellman. 2002. *The internet in everyday life.* Oxford, UK: Blackwell.

Hord, S. M. 1997. *Professional learning communities: Communities of continuous inquiry and improvement.* Austin, TX: Southwest Educational Development Laboratory. Available at *www.sedl.org/pubs/catalog/items/cha34.html*

Huffman, J., and C. Hipp. 2003. *Re-culturing schools as professional learning communities.* Lanhan, MD: Scarecrow Education.

Jonassen, D. H. 1999. Designing constructivist learning environments. In *Instructional design theories and models, Vol. 2: A new paradigm of instructional technology*, ed. C. M. Reigeluth, 215–239. Mahwah, NJ: Lawrence Erlbaum.

Jones, D. 2007. *Celebrate what's right with the world.* (VHS tape.) Available at *www.starthrower.com*

Chapter 8

Lambert, L. 2003. *Leadership capacity for lasting school improvement.* Alexandria, VA: Association for Supervision and Curriculum Development.

Lee, V. E., and J. B. Smith. 1996. Collective responsibility for learning and its effects on gains in achievement for early secondary school students. *American Journal of Education* 104: 109–146.

Leithwood, K., K. Seashore Louis, S. Anderson, and K. Wahlstrom. 2004. *How leadership influences student learning.* New York: The Wallace Foundation.

Lieberman, A., and L. Miller. 1990. Restructuring schools: What matters and what works. *Phi Delta Kappan* 71: 759–764.

Lieberman, A., and L. Miller. 2007. Transforming professional development: Understanding and organizing learning communities. In *The keys to effective schools: Educational reform as continuous improvement,* ed. W. D. Hawley, 99–116. Thousand Oaks, CA: Corwin Press.

Loucks-Horsley, S., N. Love, K. E. Stiles, S. Mundry, and P. Hewson. 2003. *Designing professional development for teachers of science and mathematics.* 2nd ed. Thousand Oaks, CA: Corwin Press.

Louis, K., S. Kruse, and H. Marks. 1996. School-wide professional community: Teachers' work, intellectual quality, and commitment. In *Authentic achievement: Restructuring schools for intellectual character,* eds. F. Newmann and Associates, 179–203. San Francisco: Jossey-Bass.

Malhoit, G., and N. Gottoni, eds. 2003. The rural school funding report. *The Rural Education Finance Center* 2: 12.

Marzano, R. J., T. Waters, and B. A. McNulty. 2005. *School leadership that works: From research to results.* Alexandria, VA: Association for Supervision and Curriculum Development.

McKean, K., and T. Fredman. 2008. *K20 science professional development institute: Year three implementation and outcomes evaluation report.* Cushing, OK: Oklahoma Technical Assistance Center.

National Research Council (NRC). 1996. *National science education standards.* Washington, DC: National Academy Press.

Newmann, F. M. 2007. Improving achievement for all students: The meaning of staff shared understanding and commitment. In *The keys to effective schools: Educational reform as continuous improvement,* ed. W. D. Hawley, 33–50. Thousand Oaks, CA: Corwin Press.

Newmann, F. M., and G. G. Wehlage. 1995. *Successful school restructuring: A report to the public and educators.* Madison, WI: Center on Organization and Restructuring of Schools, School of Education, University of Wisconsin—Madison.

Newmann, F. M., A. S. Bryk, and J. K. Nagoka. 2001. *Authentic intellectual work and standardized tests: Conflict or coexistence?* Chicago: Consortium on Chicago School Research.

O'Hair, M. J., and W. Veugelers. 2005. The case for network learning. In *Network learning for educational change,* eds. W. Veugelers and M. J. O'Hair, 1–16. Maidenhead, UK: Open University Press.

O'Hair, M. J., H. J. McLaughlin, and U. C. Reitzug. 2000. *The foundation of democratic education.* Fort Worth, TX: Harcourt Brace.

Printy, S. M. 2008. Leadership for teacher learning: A community of practice perspective. *Educational Administration Quarterly* 44 (2): 187–226.

Printy, S. M., and H. M. Marks. 2006. Shared leadership for teacher and student learning. *Theory Into Practice* 45 (2): 125–132.

Riel, M., and K. Fulton. 2001. The role of technology in supporting learning communities. *Phi Delta Kappan* 82: 518.

Roeser, R. W., C. Midgley, and T. Urdan. 1996. Perceptions of the school psychological environment and early adolescents' self-appraisals and academic engagement: The mediating role of goals and belonging. *Journal of Educational Psychology* 88: 408–422.

Schein, E. H. 2004. *Organizational culture and leadership.* 3rd ed. San Francisco: Jossey-Bass.

Schmoker, M. 1999. *Results: The key to continuous school improvement.* 2nd ed. Alexandria, VA: Association for Supervision and Curriculum Development.

Schmoker, M. 2006. *Results now: How we can achieve unprecedented improvements in teaching and learning.* Alexandria, VA: Association for Supervision and Curriculum Development.

Sergiovanni, T. J. 1994. *Building community in schools.* San Francisco: Jossey-Bass.

Sergiovanni, T. 2001. *The principalship: A reflective practice perspective.* 4th ed. Needham Heights, MA: Allyn and Bacon/Longman Publishing.

Sergiovanni, T. J. 2005. *Strengthening the heartbeat: Leading and learning together in schools.* San Francisco: Jossey-Bass.

Smith, J. B., V. E. Lee, and F. M. Newmann. 2001. *Instruction and achievement in Chicago elementary schools.* Chicago: Consortium on Chicago School Research.

Spaulding, C. 2008. Area test scores higher. *Muskogee Phoenix.* October 30. *www.muskogeephoenix.com/local/local_story_304230650.html*

Spillane, J. P., R. Halverson, and J. B. Diamond. 1999. *Toward a theory of leadership practice: A distributed perspective.* Evanston, IL: Northwestern University, Institute of Policy Research.

Wasley, P. 2002. Small classes, small schools: The time is now. *Educational Leadership* 59 (5): 6–10.

Weber, M. 1947. *The theory of social and economic organization.* Glencoe, IL: Free Press.

Wells, C., and L. Feun. 2007. Implementation of learning community principles: A study of six high schools. *NASSP Bulletin* 91: 141–160.

Chapter 8

Wenger, E. 1998. *Communities of practice: Learning, meaning and identity.* New York: Cambridge University Press.

Williams, L. A., L. Atkinson, J. Cate, and M. J. O'Hair. 2008. Mutually supportive relationships between learning community development and technology integration impact school practice and student achievement. *Theory Into Practice Journal* 47 (4): 294–302.

Yair, G. 2000. Reforming motivation: How the structure of instruction affects students' learning experiences. *British Educational Research Journal* 26 (2): 191–210.

Appendix

Resources for Professional Learning Communities

National Science Teachers Association (NSTA) Resources

NSTA Conferences: NSTA holds three area conferences and one national conference each year. Specific conference strands, professional development institutes (PDIs), and research dissemination conferences (RDCs) provide opportunities for science educators to learn about new ideas they can bring back to their PLC groups to support science learning. Information about NSTA conferences is available at *www.nsta.org/conferences*.

NSTA Learning Center: PLC members can purchase electronic copies of journal articles or individual book chapters on topics relevant to their PLCs. The NSTA Learning Center can be accessed at *http://learningcenter.nsta.org*.

NSTA Position Statements: NSTA position statements provide recommendations on key areas of concern to the science education community. PLC groups may find these position statements useful when addressing critical issues related to student learning.

NSTA Press Publications: NSTA Press publishes a variety of books for K–16 science educators. NSTA Press books can be used by PLC groups to support their professional development through book studies, access to professional information and resources, and strategies that enhance the functioning of a PLC group. NSTA Press books are listed and described at *www.nsta.org/store*. Recent NSTA Press books (published or co-published by NSTA) that may be useful to PLC groups examining effective teaching and learning include the following:

Appendix

Assessing Science Learning: Perspectives From Research and Practice, 2008, edited by Janet Coffey, Rowena Douglas, and Carole Stearns. This collection of 22 chapters, written by distinguished science educators and researchers, provides a source of professional readings for PLC groups exploring the link between assessment and student learning.

Everyday Science Mysteries, 2008, and ***More Everyday Science Mysteries,*** 2009, by Richard Konicek-Moran. These mystery stories provide a vehicle for collecting formative data PLCs can use to examine students' learning through inquiry and monitoring for conceptual change. The teacher background notes provide valuable information on students' ideas and constructivist learning.

Exemplary Science Series K–4, 5–8, and 9–12, 2005 and 2006, edited by Robert Yager. The three books in this series describe successful programs that meet the criteria of "exemplary science." The programs described in the books provide PLCs with new ideas for improving science teaching and learning.

Interpreting Assessment Data: Statistical Techniques You Can Use, 2009, by Edwin Christmann and John Badgett. This book provides suggestions PLC groups can use to interpret student assessments and results.

Learning Science and the Science of Learning, 2002, edited by Rodger Bybee. This collection of articles written by researchers and practitioners can help PLCs explore the current research on learning.

Linking Science and Literacy in the K–8 Classroom, 2006, edited by Rowena Douglas, Michael Klentschy, Karen Worth, and Wendy Binder. This collection of chapters written by NSF-funded researchers and practitioners can support PLCs looking at ways to link science with language literacy.

NSTA Tool Kit for Teaching Evolution, 2008, by Judy Elgin Jensen. This book is useful to biology teachers in a PLC examining scientific, legal, and ethical issues for teaching biological evolution.

Science as Inquiry in the Secondary Setting, 2008, edited by Julie Luft, Randy Bell, and Julie Gess-Newsome. This collection of chapters by leading researchers can help middle and secondary school PLCs explore how to incorporate more inquiry-based practices into teaching.

Science Curriculum Topic Study: Bridging the Gap Between Research and Practice, 2005, by Page Keeley. This book offers a systematic process, funded by the National

Science Foundation (NSF), that PLCs can use to make the connection between science standards and research on learning to inform curriculum, instruction, and assessment.

Science for English Language Learners: K–12 Classroom Strategies, 2006, edited by Ann Fathman and David Crowther. This book can help PLCs explore issues related to linguistically and culturally diverse students.

Science Formative Assessment: 75 Practical Strategies for Linking Assessment, Instruction, and Learning, 2008, by Page Keeley. This book provides PLC groups with information on linking assessment, instruction, and learning. The formative assessment classroom techniques (FACTs) can be used to target learning problems identified by the PLC, tried out by PLC members, and examined for their impact on learning. The book also includes a chapter on using FACTs in a PLC context.

Teaching High School Science Through Inquiry: A Case Study Approach, 2005, by Douglas Llewellyn. This book is useful to high school PLC groups looking at improving teaching and learning through inquiry.

Technology in the Secondary Science Classroom, 2008, edited by Randy Bell, Julie Gess-Newsome, and Julie Luft. This book can help middle and high school PLCs explore the potential of technology-based teaching strategies to improve learning.

Uncovering Student Ideas in Science (Volumes 1, 2, 3, and 4), 2005, 2007, 2008, and 2009, by Page Keeley and co-authors. These books provide a source of assessment probes PLCs can use to examine student thinking. The teacher notes provide PLC groups with valuable information on the probes' connections to standards and research on learning.

Using Science Notebooks in Elementary Classrooms, 2008, by Michael Klentschy. This book is a valuable guide for PLC groups implementing and studying the use of science notebooks.

The list provided here is just a sampling of NSTA Press books that could be used by PLCs to build a common knowledge base and enhance the learning of the group. To find additional NSTA books that connect to the purpose and goals of your PLC, check the NSTA website.

Appendix

PLC Website

Additional information on PLCs is available at the website All Things PLC, *www. allthingsplc.info*. This is a comprehensive website that includes research, articles, data, and tools on PLCs. It is based on the work and books of Dr. Richard DuFour and his collaborators.

On the site you will find a PLC blog and discussion board. DuFour and other PLC staff answer questions posted to their web board. The site also contains background information on the history of PLCs, articles and research, tools and resources, and evidence of effectiveness. A PLC Locator allows you to provide information on your school to be matched to schools similar to yours that have PLCs. You can read about how different PLCs work, which strategies have proved effective, and how you can get more information. The website also has archives of audio recordings of PLC panel discussions and several videos with highlights of PLC sessions. Tools on the website include those for using DuFour's Pyramid of Interventions, SMART (Specific, Measurable, Achievable, Relevant, and Time-bound) Goals tools, information on how to find time for collaborative work, and strategies for using data to inform practice.

Contributors

Linda Atkinson, Associate Director of STEM Partnerships, K20 Center, University of Oklahoma, Norman, OK

Marilyn Carlson, Professor of Mathematics Education, Department of Mathematics and Statistics, Arizona State University, Tempe, AZ

Jean M. Cate, Associate Director for Academic and University Partnerships, K20 Center, University of Oklahoma, Norman, OK

Karen Cerwin, Regional Director, K–12 Alliance, WestEd, Santa Ana, CA

Kathryn DiRanna, Director, K–12 Alliance, WestEd, Santa Ana, CA

Susan Gomez-Zwiep, Regional Director, K–12 Alliance, Science Education, California State University, Long Beach, Long Beach, CA

Page Keeley, Senior Science Program Director, Maine Mathematics and Science Alliance, Augusta, ME; President, National Science Teachers Association (2008–2009)

Carolyn Landel, Project Director, North Cascades and Olympic Science Partnership, Western Washington University, Bellingham, WA

Dan Lauffer, Senior Outreach Program Manager, University of Wisconsin—Madison, Madison, WI

Hedi Baxter Lauffer, Senior Outreach Specialist, University of Wisconsin—Madison, Madison, WI

Gregory MacDougall, Science Specialist, Ruth Patrick Science Education Center, University of South Carolina Aiken, Aiken, SC

Contributors

Susan Mundry, Associate Director, Mathematics, Science, and Technology Program, WestEd, Woburn, MA

George Nelson, Director of Science, Mathematics and Technology Education, Western Washington University, Bellingham, WA

Michael Oehrtman, Assistant Professor of Mathematics Education, Department of Mathematics and Statistics, Arizona State University, Tempe, AZ

Mary John O'Hair, Vice Provost, Director of K20 Center, and Professor of Educational Leadership, University of Oklahoma, Norman, OK

Sandra Plyley, Assistant Principal, Ben Davis High School, Metropolitan School District of Wayne Township, Indianapolis, IN

Janis Slater, Science Program Coordinator, K20 Center, University of Oklahoma, Norman, OK

John W. Somers, Director of Graduate Programs, School of Education, University of Indianapolis, Indianapolis, IN

Katherine E. Stiles, Senior Program Associate, Mathematics, Science, and Technology Program, WestEd, Indianapolis, IN

Jo Topps, Regional Director, K–12 Alliance, WestEd, Long Beach, CA

Jo Anne Vasquez, Vice President and Program Director, Arizona Transition Years Teacher and Curriculum Initiatives, Helios Education Foundation, Phoenix, AZ

Index

Index

Index

Index